About the author

Jon Robins writes about legal ... *Independent* and is contributing editor of *The Lawyer* magazine; he also writes for specialist and trade magazines.

Jon has been a legal journalist for seven years and in that time he has written more articles than he cares to remember about the problems that people have in enforcing their legal rights. Over recent years, he has seen at first hand how the drastic erosion of Legal Aid has denied many ordinary people access to justice and how the introduction of 'no win, no fee' arrangements has had mixed results for many consumers. For these reasons he has written this consumer guide on funding legal actions.

Contents

Acknowledgements

I would like to take the opportunity to thank all the people who helped in the preparation of *Affordable Law* – those who were on hand to help with background information, and those who kindly checked and read all or parts of the book. This book would not have been possible without them.

Some people deserve a special mention. Many thanks to Fiona Bawdon (Independent Lawyer); Geoffrey Bignell (partner at Just Employment solicitors); Martin Cockx and Andrew Twambley (partners at Amelans solicitors); Jim Diamond (of Legal Budgets); Aviva Golden (barrister and author of *The Daily Telegraph*'s Everyday Law series); Mark Harvey (secretary of the Association of Personal Injury Lawyers and partner at Hugh James solicitors); the Law Society press office; David Marshall (president of the Association of Personal Injury Lawyers and senior partner at Anthony Gold solicitors); Geoff Negus (Information Officer at the Office for the Supervision of Solicitors); Richard Shand (press officer at the Legal Services Commission); Tessa Shepperson (author of Lawpack's *Legal Advice Handbook* and solicitor at TJ Shepperson solicitors); Bob Tanner (of the Association of Law Costs Draftsmen); David Terry (at Terry & Co solicitors) and Kerry Underwood (senior partner at Underwoods).

In particular, Mark Harvey wrote 'Is your lawyer up to the job? A checklist' in chapter 1, David Marshall provided the 'Three examples of CFAs' in chapter 4 and David Terry wrote the 'Divorce' section in chapter 6.

I would also like to take the opportunity to say how much I appreciate the support and help of my editor Jamie Ross and assistant editor Jane Perris at Lawpack.

Finally, many thanks to Juliet and Bea.

Jon Robins

Introduction

What do you know about the law, finding a lawyer or getting legal advice? This book is a guide to help you find the best possible advice at the best possible price – if, indeed, you have to pay at all.

First of all, a note on the structure of the book. *Affordable Law* is aimed directly at the consumer who is looking for legal help. However, it also seeks to provide enough detailed information to be of use to lawyers, legal advisers in community centres, law centres and Citizens Advice Bureaux (CABs). It does not offer legal advice.

■ The right person for the job: a guide to lawyers and non-lawyers (chapter 1)

If you have a legal problem, it does not automatically follow that you need a lawyer. But if you do, this chapter explains what lawyers (and other legally qualified people) are, how to find the best and how to get the best out of them. There are also many ways of receiving sensible legal advice without having to pay for it – this chapter tells you how.

■ Keeping costs down: how to control legal expense (chapter 2)

One reason for writing this book is the alarming growth of the legal 'poverty gap', where people find themselves excluded from Legal Aid and unable (or unwilling) to pay for a lawyer. It is with an understandable sense of trepidation that prospective clients enter a solicitor's office these days. There are plenty of relics from the legal world stuck in a 1950s' mindset in their fusty old offices up and down the high streets of England and Wales, for whom legal fees are the clients' problem. But look around, and many more will offer competitive and innovative solutions.

Private fee paying is the most common and least popular way as far as the public is concerned of paying lawyers. There is a widespread suspicion (often misplaced) that the taxi meter starts running sooner than is strictly necessary.

Using this arrangement, you agree to be personally responsible for the various costs that your solicitor clocks up during the life of a claim. Solicitors charge an hourly rate, according to their level of seniority, for the work they do for you. Your solicitor will also have to make payments for other expenses on your behalf (such as expert witness reports, police reports and barrister's fees).

These costs mount up but with a responsible solicitor and careful monitoring on your part, you should never be surprised by their bill. Growing commercial pressure means that lawyers are far more amenable to providing more user-friendly ways of funding actions, such as fixed fees, which offer clients financial certainty.

■ Legal Aid: are you eligible? (chapter 3)

Clients still often walk into their solicitor's office or CAB armed with only a vague notion that if they have a good case Legal Aid will somehow cover their situation. In some cases it will, but in many cases it won't.

It has been only three years since the government launched the biggest overhaul of the Legal Aid system in its 50-year history. Fed up with an ever-spiralling Legal Aid budget, ministers cut public funding in nearly all consumer and debt cases and introduced a new, more swingeing, form of means testing where it remained available. Consequently, there is no public money for straight-forward personal injury. It is very much a stripped down service nowadays covering mainly family, social welfare problems, immigration and mental health advice. However, it does cover legal representation for people accused of crimes.

Basically, there are three questions to ask yourself to determine if your case comes under public funding:

- Are you eligible?
- Is the type of case covered by the scheme?

- Can you find a legal adviser who will take your case on?

A common misconception about Legal Aid is that it is free. If you win, you may have to pay back the money that you have paid for your solicitor.

■ No win, no fee: conditional fees and contingency fees explained (chapter 4)

New Labour's big idea was to fill the gap left by Legal Aid by expanding the pre-existing no win, no fee (NWNF) arrangements or conditional fee agreements (CFAs). Put simply, a basic CFA allows your lawyer to take the risk of running a case, so if he loses he gets nothing, but if he wins he can double his normal fee. Although a party will still have to pay the other side's legal costs if he loses, one can buy insurance to cover this cost. New Labour relaunched CFAs to ensure greater consumer benefit by allowing a party to recover from the other side the costs of insurance together with the lawyer's enhanced fee if he wins. The government then took away public funding from personal injury cases in one fell swoop.

Whilst this may sound straightforward, this brave new world has been marked by consumer scares. 'Legal market capitalism', as one commentator has called it, has led to an influx of non-lawyer entrepreneurs with some pretty mixed results. Witness the antics of the claims companies the old Claims Direct and The Accident Group (TAG), both former market leaders, which have now collapsed following huge controversy over their conduct. There are legions of well-publicised stories of accident victims losing the vast part of their damages through expensive deals, but for many this has proved a cheap (and often free) way of bringing a legal action.

Another form of NWNF is a contingency arrangement. This is where the lawyer takes a cut of your damages (e.g. one third). In most areas of the law such an approach is not allowed (the idea of taking a share of the spoils is generally frowned upon by lawyers) but it is permitted for legal advice where court action is not involved and, for example, in tribunals (especially employment tribunals).

■ Other sources of legal help: legal expenses insurance and unions (chapter 5)

There are other ways of accessing legal advice – often without paying. For example, there are thousands of insurance policies, buried in the small print on the back of your car or household insurance policies, that may cover legal advice for an action for unfair dismissal or a slip and trip case. You may not even know that you have bought the policy – and many thousands of people don't – but nonetheless it could give you access to a first-rate lawyer.

You may be one of 17 million policyholders (at last count) in the UK who have such insurance. Lawyers are now obliged to help find out if their clients have such a policy before signing off a NWNF policy.

If you are a member of a union, you may well be entitled to legal representation. There are seven million people in the country who are union members and many offer legal advice not only to card-carrying members but also to their families. Most unions will represent their members before an employment tribunal, or advise on an injury at work.

■ Life without lawyers: keeping out of the courts and DIY law (chapter 6)

Do you actually need a lawyer at all? There are plenty of ways to resolve a dispute without recourse to a solicitor. The law should always be a last resort. Many disagreements can be sorted out without the help of the legal profession. This chapter deals with how to complain effectively.

If you have a dispute with a company and it doesn't respond to your letters and enquiries, it may belong to a trade association that runs its own complaint scheme.

There has been a significant increase in 'DIY law' as it's known – mainly out of necessity as a result of the Legal Aid crisis (see chapter 3), but also because of the success of the Small Claims Court which is geared to non-lawyers. There is also a trend for legal DIY enthusiasts to complete the more basic form-filling legal processes, such as drafting Wills and even divorces, rather than paying lawyers for what is sometimes perceived, rightly or wrongly, as straightforward paperwork.

■ What to do if it all goes wrong (chapter 7)

The final chapter deals with what to do if you are not happy with your solicitor or legal adviser.

Compensation culture: myth or reality?

We are forever being told in the press that, as a society, we are in the grip of a new US-style compensation culture where greedy lawyers pursue unworthy claims to the general detriment of the rest of us. From a cynic's point of view, it may appear that there has never been a better time for bringing a legal action.

It is easy to be left with the impression that we are presently engulfed in a rising tide of litigation. But for all the talk of 'compensation culture', most of us relish the prospect of talking to a lawyer about as much as we may delight at the prospect of a visit to the dentist or an accountant – possibly both rolled into one. It could hurt and it is almost definitely going to cost you a lot of money.

Nonetheless, the newspapers claim that we have become a nation of 'slippers and trippers' obsessed with pursuing worthless claims in the courts. How do you feel about police officers suing for stress? Or perhaps your child's school has cancelled a harmless trip to the zoo because they are worried about being sued? These are the staple examples cited as evidence of our obsession with suing.

Nor is it just tabloid editorials that have come to this depressing conclusion. No less a social commentator than the Prince of Wales recently hit out at the prospect of a nation of complainers. In a letter to the then Lord Chancellor, Prince Charles complained of his 'dread' of 'the very real and growing prospect of a US-style personal injury 'culture' becoming ever more prevalent in this country. Such a culture can only lead ultimately, to...an atmosphere of distrust and suspicion, let alone the real fear of taking decisions that might lead to legal action,' he said.

A fair point you may think. However, there have been reports which suggest that we are not as litigious a society as those critics would like us to believe. For example, it was recently estimated that out of a potential 1.8 million personal injury claims a year, only 614,000 complaints were made to insurers [source: *Market Analyst Datamonitor 2002*]. So, some have argued, the situation could be a whole lot worse. The same research group also forecasted the rate at which claims were expected to increase over the next few years and came to the conclusion that complaints would only rise to 627,000 over the next five years. As an aside, whilst the number of claims may be well below the potential and not rising, the cost of claims has unquestionably shot up. For example, the cost of clinical negligence actions against the National Health Service was £446 million in 2001/02, having risen from £4 million in 1974/75 [source: *Chief Medical Officer's Report 'Making Amends' 2003*].

The more considered commentators observe that we are not on the path to US-style excess for the simple reason that on this side of the Atlantic the judge, and not the jury, keeps a tight rein on legal actions.

Clearly this is not the whole story. To take a snapshot of a different side of the legal system, employers complain that they are held to ransom by aggrieved workers and ex-workers. In the last ten years, the number of claims coming before the employment tribunals has increased threefold to around 130,000 applications a year in 2002. Bosses complain that many are without merit. For example, one survey found that applicants withdrew almost one quarter of all their claims before even reaching the tribunal [source: *The Engineering Employers' Federation 2002*].

Some of this change in culture is a direct response to the policies of successive governments that have amounted to a slow strangling of Legal Aid. For example, it was New Labour's decision to abolish Legal Aid in 1999 in personal injury cases, together with its bolstering of NWNF, that paved the way for claims companies. They then drummed up millions of claims through saturation TV advertising campaigns and by sending out armies of agents onto the high streets of the UK.

But the flip side of this debate is that we, as a society, are becoming more willing to exercise our rights as consumers and workers. If you are the victim of a botched hospital operation, why should you suffer in silence? Why should your boss sack you on some flimsy pretext when you really know that he wants to make way for a younger model? The vast majority of people that seek legal advice are genuine and sincere.

No win, no fee...no problem?

Despite the myth that litigation is somehow an easy option, the reality is very different. If, for example, you are recovering from a bad car crash in which you were an innocent passenger or, perhaps, you have recently lost your job for no good reason, finding a lawyer (if that is what you need) and obtaining the right legal advice can seem a daunting, if not impossible, task.

In essence, this book seeks to demystify the process. Take the example of NWNF arrangements (or conditional fees) which have proved so controversial. This phrase has, for better or worse, firmly lodged itself in the public consciousness and also has become widely misunderstood. NWNF has proved unpopular with the press who blame it for prompting a deluge of unmerited claims but, more importantly, it has proved treacherous for many accident victims who have seen their well-deserved damages swallowed up by legal claims.

The story of Jason (as told in *The Sun* newspaper) provides a cautionary tale about the state of access to justice today. Jason worked in a bar and was scarred for life after he was instructed to empty a tea urn full of boiling water that did not have proper handles. His case was handled by a claims company that has since gone bankrupt. After a two-year wait Jason was awarded £1,525, only to receive a cheque for £63, with the rest going to the claims company, its agents and lawyers. Jason's accident was clearly his own misfortune, although his claim was handled for the benefit of everyone else involved. This should never have happened for a number of reasons: Jason could have been covered by legal expenses insurance (LEI), or perhaps he was a member of a union who offered legal advice. If not, had Jason consulted a competent solicitor he could have guaranteed that most or all of the damages would have come to him intact.

If there is a wider lesson to be learned regarding the mixed results of no win, no fee, perhaps it is that consumers shouldn't just place themselves unthinkingly in the hands of other legal advisers but must make the informed choice for themselves.

Chapter 1
The right person for the job
A guide to lawyers and non-lawyers

Finding a lawyer isn't difficult. After all, there is no shortage. There are 68,466 solicitors today working in 9,743 firms throughout the UK – from dusty rooms above shops on the nation's high streets to swanky office blocks in the City. There were only 25,366 solicitors 30 years ago, which is either an alarming or a comforting thought depending on your point of view. There are also many lawyers and legal advisers working in other advice centres, including 2,000 Citizens Advice Bureaux (CABs) and 52 law centres. The problem is not finding a lawyer, but finding the right one for the job if, indeed, you need a lawyer at all.

Finding the right advice for your particular problem is absolutely crucial. To begin with, you should always discover as much as possible about the nature of any dispute you are involved in and your legal rights. Clearly, you do not want to run up lawyers' fees unnecessarily, nor do you want to pay for what amounts to mere hand holding. A survey for *Which? Magazine* once revealed that nearly half of those with legal problems consulted solicitors, despite the fact that they were often charged for legal advice, and only one fifth used the free services of a law centre or a CAB. Even fewer relied on their legal expenses insurance (LEI) or contacted trading standards departments for local consumer complaints. If you do use a solicitor, you should make sure that you avail yourself of a free introductory interview if possible. But there is a wealth of other resources – especially if you have access to the Internet.

Different sources of advice

People frequently talk about 'lawyers' without understanding exactly who or what they are dealing with. It is a generic term incorporating people with vastly different skills and qualifications – from the non-qualified paralegals, to the highly specialised solicitor or the courtroom barrister. The reason why it is important to be able to make a distinction is because different 'lawyers' have various levels of competence and offer different levels of consumer protection.

A further word of warning: there will be plenty of people willing to offer you 'legal advice' regarding the merits of your claim who have absolutely no training in the law.

You should be aware of the different types of lawyer.

■ Solicitors

Most solicitors work in private practice mainly in law firms, which are partnerships, or else as sole practitioners (SPs) if it is one lawyer working without partners. There are two sorts of partners in a law firm: equity partners, who own the firm and take a share of the profits, and the less senior salaried partners. The other solicitors are called 'assistants', sometimes referred to as 'associates'. Within the business, the solicitors are known as 'fee-earners' because they have contact with the client and do the work that generates the income. Many other solicitors are employed in business, local government and the civil service.

Generally speaking, it is barristers that represent individuals in court. However, since 1994, solicitors have been entitled to the same rights of audience (i.e. they can appear before the courts) provided that they are sufficiently experienced.

The growth of 'solicitor-advocates' (as they are known) in the profession has been slow but steady. The total number of solicitors in 2003 with higher court rights of audience is around 1,800, which is already about 16 per cent of the practising Bar. Clearly, there are consumer benefits if your solicitor can handle himself in the courtroom without taking on the expense of external counsel.

See 'The solicitor explained' on page 25 for more information.

■ Barristers

Barristers (who are also called 'counsel', which is always used in the singular) are specialist legal advisers and courtroom advocates. There are more than 10,000 barristers in the UK. They have to pass a qualifying law degree, a professional examination and serve one year in 'pupillage' (i.e. the training period after they have completed the academic side of their education) either 'in chambers' (i.e. self-employed) or in employment.

Barristers (when practising as barristers, as opposed to working as employed lawyers in larger organisations) are self-employed and practise in chambers where they share accommodation and administration costs. They must also be members of one of the four Inns of Court: Gray's Inn, Lincoln's Inn, Inner Temple and Middle Temple. The Inns are also responsible for providing everything from continuing education to running disciplinary tribunals for their members.

The most senior barristers are known as 'Queen's Silk' (QCs). These are barristers who have accepted the invitation of the Lord Chancellor to join the top rank of the profession by 'taking silk' (i.e. swapping their plain cotton gowns for the smarter and pricier silk versions). Hence, QCs are also known as 'silks'.

Silks are very much under attack at the moment not least from the Office of Fair Trading, which in a recent report on anti-competitive practices in the professions concluded that they were of 'questionable' value to consumers. The charge against silks is that they act as 'a self-perpetuating price-rigging cartel' (as the Labour MP and solicitor Andrew Dismore put it). Critics argue that the QC title allows an elite band of the profession to hike fees up overnight once they have been appointed. Another complaint is the shadowy appointment process whereby the Lord Chancellor takes 'secret soundings' (as they are known) from the profession as to who is and who isn't worthy. By contrast, the Bar staunchly defends the QC system as a 'kitemark of quality', or a consumer seal of approval to help solicitors find the best advocates for their clients' cases. It remains to be seen how long the QC rank lasts.

Generally, barristers have no direct dealings with the public and for this reason this chapter will mainly consider solicitors. (There is a scheme called 'BarDIRECT' whereby organisations or individuals who are suitable to instruct barristers, because they have expertise in particular areas of the law, can apply to the Bar Council to be licensed to instruct barristers directly in those areas.)

The barristers' governing body is the Bar Council. To find out more, go to www.barcouncil.org.uk.

■ Other advisers

There are many other people who provide legal advice both within law firms and outside of them. When you instruct a firm of solicitors, it is good practice to check the client care letter (see page 57 for further information) to find out to what extent work may be delegated.

Failure to send a client care letter by your solicitor means that he may not be allowed to charge for his services. In one case (*Pearless De Rougemont & Co v Stuart John Pilbrow, 17 March 1999*), the court held that because there was no client care letter, it was implied that there was a contract for legal services to be provided by a solicitor. In that particular instance, 80 per cent of the family work was undertaken by a paralegal. The court held that the client did not have to pay his legal bill because he was not made aware of the status of his adviser.

You should always be aware of what qualifications your adviser has. Is he regulated by a governing body, and does he have professional indemnity insurance and a complaints procedure?

Legal executives

There are 22,000 legal executives and they are qualified lawyers specialising in a particular area of law. They will have passed the Institute of Legal Executives (ILEX) professional qualification in an area of legal practice to the same level as that required of solicitors. They will have at least five years' experience of working under the supervision of a solicitor and are issued with an annual practising certificate.

Legal executives can handle the legal aspects of a property transfer, assist in the formation of a company, deal with actions before the High Court or County courts, draft Wills, as well as advise in criminal and family law.

Like solicitors, they are regarded as 'fee earners' and their work is charged directly to clients. This is an important difference between legal executives and other types of legal support staff.

To find out more, visit the Institute of Legal Executives' website at www.ilex.org.uk.

Paralegals

Paralegals undertake legal work without any formal legal qualification. Having said that, in some cases they can be more experienced than the professionally qualified solicitors they work alongside. (Paralegals used to be called 'solicitors' clerks'.)

Trainee solicitors

Lawyers who are undergoing the final practical stage of their training within a law firm. (Trainee solicitors used to be known as 'articled clerks'.)

Licensed conveyancers

Licensed conveyancers are specialist property lawyers, trained and qualified in all aspects of the law dealing with property. Conveyancing was the sole responsibility of solicitors until 1987.

They are recognised by financial institutions such as banks and lenders. Many licensed conveyancers practise on their own or in partnership. After the examinations and the practical training requirements have been undertaken, they can apply for a licence that allows them to offer conveyancing services as an employed person. Once they have held an employed licence for three years, they can apply for a full licence to offer conveyancing services directly to the public.

They are required to purchase professional indemnity insurance and comply with the rules of the profession, such as sending a written estimate at the outset of a transaction.

See the Council for Licensed Conveyancers' website at www. conveyancer.org.uk.

■ Unqualified legal advice

As mentioned before, there are legions of unregulated and non-legally qualified claims advisers who pursue compensation claims taking a slice of the damages in employment or personal injury claims. Usually they work on a no win, no fee (NWNF) basis, taking a percentage of the settlement. If a case becomes contentious (i.e. if it is going to court), the matter has to be referred on to a solicitor. You should be very wary. It is not likely that they will have any professional training; nor will they offer any complaints procedure; nor provide the protection of professional indemnity insurance.

■ Free legal advice

There are various sources of free legal advice, for example, CABs, housing advice centres, money advice centres and law centres. Central to New Labour's reform of publicly funded legal advice was to harness the huge and disparate 'not for profit' sector.

Citizens Advice Bureaux

The National Association of Citizens Advice Bureaux (NACAB) claims to help solve nearly six million new problems every year. It offers free legal advice mainly on debt and consumer issues, benefits, housing, legal matters, employment and immigration. Advisers can also help, for example, by filling out forms, writing letters or negotiating with creditors. They can also point you in the direction of a solicitor.

There are 2,000 CAB outlets in the UK with nearly 25,000 people working in the Citizens Advice service of which the vast majority (79 per cent) are lawyers.

To contact your nearest CAB write, drop in or telephone during opening hours. For more advice, see their website at www.nacab.org.uk.

Law centres

There are at present 52 law centres, 20 of which are in London, providing a free and independent professional legal service to people who live or work in their catchment areas. They specialise in the law relating to welfare rights, immigration and nationality, housing and homelessness, employment rights, and sex and race discrimination. To find out more and to find out where their centres are, visit their website at www.lawcentres.org.uk.

In person and on the web

There are other sources of free legal advice such as the Solicitors Pro Bono Group (SPBG) (www.probonogroup.org.uk). Pro bono is short for 'pro bono publico' and is legal-speak for unpaid or charitable work done by lawyers. The Lord Chief Justice, Lord Woolf, believes that one reason the legal profession is not automatically associated with public-spiritedness is down to this rather archaic phrase which (he would argue) obscures the good works of lawyers. A competition was recently run for a replacement and the rather literal-sounding 'Law for Free' was the winner – it was also Lord Woolf's preferred synonym. However, this suggestion appears to have fallen somewhat flat.

The SPBG does not take on cases for individuals; nor does it issue a list of individual solicitors undertaking pro bono work. It only administers the scheme. A brand new website, www.probonouk. net, has just been launched at the time of going to press, which promises to be the 'marketplace and exchange forum' for all parties, including members of the public. It may be worth taking a look.

There is also the Free Representation Unit, a registered charity based in Greater London, which is dedicated to the provision of free legal representation for those who cannot afford paid legal representation before tribunals in areas where Legal Aid is unavailable. It specialises in employment and social security law, as well as some criminal injury compensation and immigration work. However, it does not give advice to members of the public directly. Referrals are made from advice agencies and law firms. For more information, see www.fru.org.uk. There are also groups such as the civil rights group Liberty or the homeless charity Shelter which provide specialist legal advice.

For online information that is free, the Community Legal Service (CLS) has a website www.justask.org.uk which offers a guide to online legal resources; the government-backed trading standard central website (www.tradingstandards.gov.uk) has leaflets for business and consumers (giving advice on everything from buying a second-hand car to resolving a problem with your dry-cleaners); and the CAB at www.adviceguide.org.uk has an excellent consumer-friendly site.

The law firm Thompsons, which specialises in acting for trade union clients, has a good site (www.thompsons.law.co.uk), as has the Coventry Law Centre (www.covlaw.org.uk). Both have been awarded CLS Internet Quality Marks.

A very useful site, which brings together many different sources of legal advice, is run by Delia Venables (www.venables.co.uk).

The solicitor explained

Lawyers attract more than their fair share of bad press – some of it deserved and a fair amount not. On the whole, lawyers have to meet exacting professional qualifications, comply with fairly rigorous professional regulations and take out professional insurance.

Here are a few of the consumer protections offered by solicitors:

■ Training

The training and entry requirements to the solicitors' profession are tough and competitive, taking some six years to complete. They involve passing a law degree, sitting a further professional examination and then training for two years within a law firm.

All solicitors must be on the Roll – a register of all persons qualified as solicitors. The Law Society governs admission to the Roll which is kept by the Master of the Rolls, the most senior judge in the Court of Appeal. There were 109,553 solicitors on the Roll at the beginning of 2003, not all practising. The Society is supposed to ensure that new solicitors are fit and proper persons and have undergone the relevant training.

Solicitors in private practice must hold a practising certificate issued annually by the Law Society. This guarantees that they are both qualified to practise and have insurance to protect you if anything goes wrong. You can contact the Law Society to check if a lawyer has a certificate. Once qualified, solicitors must keep up to date through a programme of continuing education.

■ Insurance

Solicitors are insured which protects their clients as well as themselves. They must have professional indemnity insurance, which covers situations where solicitors are negligent. Solicitors must also contribute to their compensation fund which ensures that if a solicitor is dishonest, the public will not suffer financially.

It is administered by the Office for the Supervision of Solicitors (OSS) (see chapter 7).

Professional rules

Solicitors are also governed by their own professional rules (published in *The Guide to the Professional Conduct of Solicitors*). Whilst it is not quite the lawyers' equivalent of the Hippocratic Oath, it provides a code of ethics that underpins the profession. These rules require, for example, that a solicitor:

- must always act in his client's interest (the only exception is when it conflicts with a solicitor's duty to uphold justice as an Officer of the Supreme Court);
- must not act if his prospective client's interests may conflict with the interests of another client, or with other interests;
- must keep his client's details confidential;
- must keep his client's money in a separate account from other money;
- may not set up on his own until he has been qualified for three years.

Controls on solicitors' fees

The legal profession is rare insofar as its fees are controlled in one form or another by Parliament and there are procedures in place for lawyers' fees to be challenged without too much difficulty, provided the challenge is mounted promptly. There are tighter restrictions on how lawyers' charge than most other businesses. For example, they are obliged to disclose to their clients any commissions received and in most cases to treat the commission as belonging to the client. As discussed before, payment by performance and no win, no fee deals are heavily regulated.

Complaints procedures

All law firms are obliged to have their own complaints procedures. There is a special arm of the Law Society, the OSS, which investigates complaints of professional misconduct and inadequate professional service. If the OSS finds that there is a serious case of misconduct to answer, the solicitor may be brought before a special court, the Solicitors Disciplinary Tribunal. If solicitors fail to abide by the rules of conduct, there are a range of penalties, from a rebuke to being struck off the Roll, which means that they can no longer work as lawyers. If solicitors fail to provide an adequate professional service, the OSS can award compensation to the client or order a solicitor to reduce his bill. See chapter 7.

To find out more, visit the Law Society website at www. lawsociety.org.uk.

How to choose the right solicitor

What type of firm to instruct?

There are 'horses for courses' in today's legal market. There is no point in just randomly selecting a firm of solicitors from your Yellow Pages. Law firms come in all shapes and sizes – from a one-man-band run from someone's living room to multinational firms based in the commercial heart of the City of London with offices across the globe. Nor should you expect the solicitor who represented you on your house move to be competent to advise you on a dispute involving your business.

The degree of specialist knowledge and rates vary accordingly. This is a guide to the various different types of firms.

■ Sole practitioners and small firms

Sole practitioners (SPs) are the solicitors who practise without other partners, although they are not necessarily on their own as they may have support staff. According to recent Law Society statistics there are 4,098 solo solicitors in the UK. Some operate like any other firm, employing other solicitors, paralegals and support staff, except for the fact that they are run by a sole solicitor and not a partnership.

Most SPs opt to work either by themselves or with a couple of support staff, usually for lifestyle reasons, preferring the relative independence and freedom that this offers. But in a small number of cases, a solicitor practises in this way simply because he cannot cut it in partnership or find a job elsewhere. It should also be pointed out that some SPs are just hanging on in there waiting for retirement (the average age is 51 years) and are somewhat resistant to change. Recent research found that of some 600 medium and small law firms, just 17 were not using personal computers – and they were all SPs.

Small firms include SPs and practices of up to five partners. Most firms in the country or in small towns are 'small'. Frequently they will be 'generalist' practices, with an emphasis on Wills and conveyancing. You will find such firms perfectly satisfactory for run-of-the-mill cases. As a general rule, you should be wary of firms that take on too much, though, so if you have a specialist concern then go and see an expert.

■ High street firms

Basically, such firms provide the backbone of the profession. They are usually of medium size, of five to 20 partners, and will cater for the local community for both businesses and individuals. The main areas of advice will be conveyancing, employment law, personal injury, family as well as basic commercial work. Many will do Legal Aid work as well, but that number is decreasing. A few years ago most firms did at least some Legal Aid work but since the introduction of the CLS and the new contracting regime there has been a move to drive out those firms that dabbled in publicly funded work. From April 2001, only law firms and other advice centres that have a contract with the Legal Services

Commission (LSC) can provide such assistance. As for advice on how to find a Legal Aid firm, see chapter 3.

The high street firms have been under attack on a number of fronts, not least by the steady erosion of Legal Aid work. But they are also feeling the pinch because of the relentless progress made by non-lawyers into what used to be their staple money earners, such as conveyancing (where they enjoyed a monopoly until the creation of licensed conveyancers). The personal injury market has also been under relentless assault from non-lawyer claims companies in the last few years. The local high street solicitor, catering for all your family's legal needs, is increasingly becoming a thing of the past, having gone the same way as the local corner shop, butcher or bank. The future does not look too bright either – see 'Tesco law' on page 30.

■ Regional and national firms

These are legal practices that have a wider geographical range. Law firms are slowly changing the way they operate to meet new consumer demand. There are obvious advantages in having a lawyer who you can pop in and see, but increasingly consumers do not expect that luxury. In many cases they do not have the choice. For example, there may not be a firm in your area that offers legally aided advice or, if you have a legal expenses insurer, it may be that its solicitor is based in a different part of the country.

Increasingly, firms with a national reach are offering 'high street' legal services. In particular, there are bulk conveyancing firms (sometimes run by estate agents) that are offering very competitive fees. There are more personal injury and employment firms that are marketing their services nationally and not just where their head office is based. From the consumer's point of view, the message has to be to shop around and find out where you can get the best value for money – it may not be around the corner.

■ Large firms and City firms

The biggest firms will have hundreds of partners and offices throughout Europe and the world. They will specialise in commercial work but will also offer their services to very wealthy individuals. As well as practising in corporate work, they will specialise in discrete areas of law, such as intellectual property, planning and tax.

'City firms' are those that are based in the City of London. Both large firms and City firms are hugely expensive (a 2003 survey revealed the average hourly rates were almost £350 for a partner and £230 for a senior assistant). This is because their services are targeted at corporate clients and the very rich.

■ 'Niche' firms

These are highly expert firms that concentrate in specialist areas of law, for example, defamation, media, employment and personal injury. As specialists they will charge more than high street firms. However, if you need expert advice on an esoteric point of law, then they may be better qualified for the job and prove cheaper in the long run. Of course, they may not offer the same 'all round advice', which may be necessary if your problem covers a number of areas of law. Take, for example, a stress at work claim that may involve a claim against an employer for unfair dismissal and a claim for personal injury. It would be sensible for one firm to cover both claims.

■ 'Tesco law'

This is shorthand for the government reforms that will allow banks, financial institutions and supermarkets to offer legal services directly to the public. The present government is keen to sweep away restrictions under which solicitors can form partnerships only with fellow lawyers. This move would completely change the landscape of legal services and it would enable you to pop down to Tesco, now the unwitting symbol of the movement, and get your Will drawn up.

This represents a huge threat to the already besieged high street profession. There are real concerns that access to publicly funded legal advice will wither on the vine if more firms pull out of Legal Aid as a result of these reforms. However, the government takes the view that the greater the competition, the better the deal for the consumer.

Where to start looking?

■ Personal knowledge or recommendation

The days of the family firm of solicitors tending to all your legal affairs are passing. Increasingly, the legal profession is becoming a profession of specialists, and so the firm of solicitors that handles your conveyancing may not have the expertise to advise you on a compensation claim. A quick phone call should establish whether it may be in a position to help you. A personal recommendation from a friend, colleague or trusted solicitor can also be useful.

■ Directories

If you are starting from scratch, the Law Society can help you identify a local solicitor. Call 0870 606 6575 or visit the website on www.solicitors-online.com, where it features an online directory listing a firm's specialisations. Yellow Pages and Thomsons' local directories in England and Wales include listings of solicitors.

If you are in business, Lawyers For Your Business (LFYB) represents some 1,400 firms of solicitors in England and Wales and is aimed at the smaller owner-managed ones. The scheme is administered by the Law Society, and backed by the likes of the Federation of Small Businesses and the Forum of Private Business. In order 'to remove the risk of incurring unexpectedly high legal costs', all LFYB members offer a free consultation, lasting at least half an hour. If you do not have a solicitor, you can contact the Law Society. It will send you a list of LFYB members in your area, and (at the time of going to press) a voucher for a free consultation.

■ Ask an expert

A law centre or CAB may be able to recommend local solicitors who are experienced in the appropriate area of law or will be able to provide information on how to find an appropriate solicitor.

How much are you prepared to pay?

You should find out how much they are likely to charge – for example, their hourly rate and fixed fee arrangements if appropriate. Price alone may not be a determining factor: a specialist may charge more but may offer better advice and prove cost effective in the long run.

Is your solicitor experienced?

■ Panel members and accreditation

If you are looking for expert legal advice, check to see if your solicitor is a member of a Quality Assured panel, set up by the Law Society to demonstrate specialist knowledge to prospective clients. The Society runs panels in family, immigration, personal injury law, clinical negligence, Children Act proceedings, mental health tribunals, family mediation and planning law. You can find a list of members on the Law Society website.

Accident Line is the Law Society's own free personal injury referral service. It puts victims of accidents, caused by someone else, in touch with a specialist personal injury solicitor near their home or work.

Other organisations such as the Association of Personal Injury Lawyers, Action for the Victims of Medical Accidents and the

Motor Accident Solicitors Society run their own accreditation schemes. There are no universal standards offered by accreditation schemes so it is worth checking how exacting membership is. It is also worth looking at the websites of other professional groups such as the Employment Lawyers Association, the Immigration Law Practitioners' Association and the Solicitors Family Law Association (see Appendix for their contact details).

Directories

For expertise in commercial law and a guide to the City law firms, there are a number of directories that are worth consulting. For example, there is *The Legal 500* (published by Legalease) and the *Chambers UK Guide to the Legal Profession* (published by Chambers & Partners, see www.chambersandpartners.com).

Lexcel

The Law Society runs its own Quality Mark called 'Lexcel', which is another indicator of a good firm. Firms that display the Lexcel logo have been independently judged to meet the Society's own practice management standards.

Legal Aid

Are you eligible for Legal Aid? You can find a local solicitor by contacting your nearest CAB or law centre. You will then have to find a law firm that does Legal Aid work. There are problems in certain parts of the country in terms of Legal Aid coverage – see chapter 3. There is a list of these firms and other advice agencies available on the CLS website (www.justask.org.uk). You can also ring the CLS Directory Line on 0845 608 1122.

Only organisations with a contract with the LSC can provide advice. This means that they have been checked to see that they meet certain standards and can provide a quality service. For some types of cases, in particular, family, immigration, mental health and clinical negligence, the organisation must not only only have a contract with the LSC but the contract must actually cover the specific type of case. So if you already have a solicitor, ask and find out if he has a contract. All firms taking part on the scheme will display a CLS logo as shown.

Community Legal Service

CLS has developed its own 'Quality Mark', another accreditation scheme, which is awarded only to organisations that pass regular quality checks carried out by the LSC. Providers who have achieved the Quality Mark will display the CLS logo in their offices. In Just Ask!'s Directory, those firms with the Quality Mark have the logo to the left of their name.

Have you been charged with a criminal offence? If a person is at a police station, or has been charged with an imprisonable offence, he can obtain free legal advice under the duty solicitors' scheme.

What are your requirements?

Not all firms will do NWNF or fixed fee arrangements, for example. So if you are interested, you will have to find a solicitor who is amenable.

If you need to see a solicitor about a personal matter you will want him to be sympathetic. You may prefer to deal with someone of the same sex, or you may feel more comfortable with a lawyer your own age. There are many firms that specialise in providing legal services to different ethnic minority groups, as well as those specifically geared to the legal needs of gays and lesbians. Don't be afraid to say that this is what you want.

Will your solicitor offer a free first interview?

First of all, bear in mind that in many cases you will be able to avail yourself of free advice from a solicitor. A direct request for unpaid legal guidance at the start of a case to identify whether it has merits and how it should best be pursued will, in most cases, be greeted positively. It is also an opportunity for you to size up your lawyer as well. Many lawyers are more approachable and less stuffy than their reputation suggests. A willingness to have a chat about your case will give you a good measure of the kind of lawyer you are dealing with. You will find that many firms advertise a free first meeting in their promotional material and on their websites.

The first meeting

Preparation

Once you have found the right firm, make an appointment. You should explain the nature of your situation and ensure that the firm is well qualified to advise. If you plan to take someone with you to your first meeting, mention this. Also ask if there is anything specific you should bring for the first meeting, such as proof of identity or income if you are applying for Legal Aid.

You should not be charged for a preliminary interview, unless substantive legal advice is offered. In fact, a free 'introductory offer' of an hour's legal advice may be all you need to resolve your problem.

You should put together all the paperwork that you think is relevant and present it in order. This will help the solicitor to understand your situation, but also you then won't end up paying him to do the filing. Spend some time thinking about what you want to say to your solicitor and the questions you want him to answer. Make notes, so that you won't forget when it comes to the meeting.

Is your lawyer up to the job? A checklist

Here are some questions to ask which should help you establish whether your lawyer is up to the job:

1. **Who is handling your case?** It is essential that you know just who is running your case. Not every lawyer you see will be a solicitor (with his professional training, regulation by the Law Society and professional indemnity insurance). It is not essential that it is a solicitor who works on your claim (it may be a paralegal or a legal executive) but it is essential that he reports to one. By contrast, claims assessors are not solicitors, are unregulated and provide little, if any, consumer protection. They also may charge considerably more than a lawyer.

2. **Can you see your lawyer at your own convenience?** The ideal situation is that you can meet your lawyer in person whenever you want, at home or in his office. However, it is becoming more difficult, particularly in the lower value claims, to go and see your lawyer. Unfortunately, this is often the price to be paid with a lawyer provided by the legal expenses insurer or trade unions. It is always better to be able to deal with a person you can see.

3. **What are your lawyer's qualifications for the job?** Ask your lawyer what qualifications he has that enables him to do the job. Find out whether he is a member of any of the Law Society's specialist panels or other specialist bodies.

4. **How many cases of this particular type has your lawyer worked on in the last two years?** Your case may be particularly complex or very simple, but that's not necessarily a judgement you can make. However, it is essential that you have the right person for the job. A clinical negligence claim is a good example of this. This is a particularly complex type of claim and requires more than just a personal injury lawyer,

however experienced or indeed competent. Ask the lawyer how many cases of this particular type he has worked on. If you are not happy with the answer, ask to see another lawyer from the organisation or look elsewhere.

5. **How many cases has your lawyer taken to a court hearing in the last two years?** A good lawyer should never be afraid to take a case to court if necessary. The present court system encourages the settlement of cases wherever possible but often the best way of avoiding court is to prepare to go to court with your opponent believing that your lawyer is prepared to take your claim there. If your lawyer has not taken a case to trial or the court doors for settlement at least within the last two years, then you should be cautious.

6. **What is your lawyer's percentage rate of success in the last two years?** The lawyer may have nice offices, his adverts may be impressive, but does he actually win his cases? All lawyers, both firms and individuals, ought to be able to tell you not only how many of your sort of case they have worked on but how many they have actually won. Any reticence in revealing this information should lead you to look elsewhere.

7. **How many cases does your lawyer work on at any one time?** The best lawyers are no better than average if they do not have the necessary time to work on your case. As a general guide lawyers involved in litigation should rarely have more than 150 cases.

8. **Have any successful complaints been made against your lawyer?** If he will not answer this question, choose another lawyer! If he tells you that he has, then you will need to form a view as to whether the number and nature of complaints should cause you to seek another lawyer.

[*checklist provided by Mark Harvey, partner at Hugh James solicitors and secretary of the Association of Personal Injury Lawyers*]

At the meeting

Check how long the meeting is scheduled to last so that you do not find your time is up before you have had a chance to make all your points.

Your solicitor will need to ask you lots of questions. Try to answer these as clearly and accurately as you can, but also be as brief as you can. Get out the notes you have made and tick off each point as it is covered.

Make sure you ask all your questions and fully understand the answers you are given. If there is anything you don't understand, ask again until you do. If it helps, make notes during the interview.

At the first meeting it is important to establish an estimate for the cost of the work and how it will be paid. Solicitors should tell you at the outset how much a case like yours is likely to cost and how they work out the costs. Make sure you discuss this with your solicitor as early as possible to set your mind at rest.

Make sure you ask your solicitor to send you a letter afterwards confirming:

- that he has taken on the work and the nature of the advice you have been given;
- the name and job title of the person in the firm who will be dealing with your case day to day;
- the time the whole business is likely to take and arrangements for progress reports;
- an estimate of your costs and any agreed spending limits;
- any more information you need to supply; and
- a contact at the firm should you have a complaint about your solicitor's service.

First meeting checklist

Here are some of the things you may want to raise at your first meeting:

- Are there better ways to solve the problem? For example, can you approach your opponent directly? It may be that mediation (where a third party helps both sides come to an agreement) or an ombudsman scheme can assist.
- What are your prospects of success?
- Does your solicitor understand your problem?
- Are you clear about costs? For example, will you have to pay the other side's costs?
- Do you understand everything that was said? Ask your solicitor to translate any 'legalese' (unfamiliar and technical words that need to be explained).
- Is your solicitor going to write confirming that he has taken on the work?
- What happens next?
- Do you need to do anything?

Maintaining a good relationship with your lawyer

It is well worth keeping on the right side of your lawyer. Solicitors are busy people and although your case may be the most important thing to you, it will be one of many cases that they will have on the go. So it is always useful to be both helpful and polite in your dealings with your lawyer. With this in mind, here are some tips:

- Give clear instructions to the solicitor. Make sure that all of your documentation is in order, preferably arranged chronologically, and that he has all the relevant information without bombarding him with useless information. In complex cases, it may be useful to write a summary of key events or a timetable.

- Always respond promptly to requests for information.
- Always pay bills and requests for money promptly – provided, of course, that they are reasonable.
- Do not withhold information or lie to your solicitor. If he finds out that you have been lying he will probably be entitled to stop acting for you.
- Remember that you are not his only client.
- Do not make unnecessary phone calls and demands on your lawyer's time. As well as annoying him, you may end up being billed for the time he takes responding to your non-productive calls.
- Listen to advice. A good lawyer will inevitably have far more experience. That does not mean you necessarily follow it, but be open-minded.

Chapter 2
Keeping costs down

How to control legal expense

A prospective client should never be embarrassed about talking about costs with a solicitor or legal adviser. And they, in turn, should never be anything less than forthcoming about the likely expense.

Urban myths of solicitors and their fondness for excessive billing abound. For example, what about the solicitor who charged for attending the wedding of his client's daughter? Actually, that one is true. The reality is that solicitors can be expensive and, if you surrender control, you may be unpleasantly surprised by a large bill.

Having said that, there are ways of keeping costs down and there is no earthly reason why a lawyer should present you with a shocking bill provided both sides communicate clearly. Certainly, the Law Society's own regulations cannot be any clearer – solicitors should explain what the likely cost is going to be and tell you if their costs are going to exceed this level.

The most common method of charging is the hourly rate, and it is the one that tends to strike fear into the heart of many prospective clients. The anxiety is that the taxi meter starts running as soon as you enter a solicitor's office. However, your solicitor will often be able to tell you at the outset of the case what its cost is going to be. Whether or not he can do this, you can still agree a method of controlling costs. For example, a solicitor may offer a fixed fee so you'll know the maximum you will have to pay. Alternatively, he may set a cost limit and agree a figure beyond which he will not go without your say-so. You can then review what to do once that point is reached – but if you are involved in court action, it may not be possible to stop. One approach you may take is to make regular payments so as to spread the cost or your solicitor can bill you for the work stage by stage.

Lawyers tend to be a fairly conservative bunch and the certainty of the hourly rate guarantees that it is their preferred choice of payment. Having said that, clients have become increasingly savvy about lawyers' fees and there are increasingly sophisticated ways of paying your lawyer to suit your means – for example, there are no win, no fee

(NWNF) and other performance-related forms of pay, as well as fixed fees. In fact, as a result of stiff competition amongst law firms there is something of a buyer's market in legal services developing. So if you don't like what is on offer at one firm, shop around.

This chapter is an explanation as to how legal costs work, how lawyers charge and how to keep costs down – and it breaks down into three sections accordingly. For what you should do if you disagree with your lawyer's bill, see chapter 7.

Legal costs explained

Basic principles

Contentious and non-contentious work

There are two types of solicitors' work. Contentious work involves legal action through the courts, and non-contentious work covers everything else. Work becomes contentious when court proceedings have actually begun – and that includes advice and preparation where proceedings are subsequently begun. (As well as court work, contentious work includes arbitration, see chapter 6.) Examples of non-contentious work are conveyancing, drawing up Wills, as well as negotiating contracts. Tribunals are considered non-contentious.

The distinction is relevant here because lawyers' rules about costs differ according to which type of work is involved.

Civil law and criminal law

Civil law concerns the rights and duties of private people and businesses in their dealings with other individuals and businesses – as opposed to criminal law which concerns offences against the law of the land and which are punishable by the state.

Again, the distinction is relevant because the costs regimes are different.

What are legal costs?

The costs of any case comprise lawyers' fees, expenses and VAT. In contentious cases there is the potential exposure not only to your own solicitor's costs but also to your opponent's.

Lawyers' fees

Traditionally, a solicitor is paid for the time he spends on a case. He will charge for telephone calls to the client and the other side's solicitor, as well as attending meetings, writing letters, reading correspondence, filling in forms and drafting documents. If there are court proceedings, then there is also the preparation of statements for the case, appearing in court, and meeting with barristers and witnesses.

Expenses

Expenses (known by lawyers as 'disbursements') can include court fees, fees paid to the Land Registry on a house move and the costs of local searches. If it is a court case there may be court fees, as well as barristers' fees, experts' fees and costs draftsmen's fees (see page 146 for further information on costs draftsmen).

VAT

VAT is charged on the sum of the fees plus those expenses that are subject to VAT (such as barristers' fees).

Costs in civil cases

■ Loser pays

The general rule in court is that the losing party pays the costs of the successful party. Or, as lawyers would have it, 'costs follow the event'.

If you win your case, the court may award you costs on the 'standard basis'. This means that the court will only allow costs that are in proportion to the matters in issue, so costs will not be recovered if a judge takes the view that your solicitor is overcharging. Any doubt as to whether costs are reasonable will be resolved in favour of the party who foots the bill. This may not necessarily be the same sum as your solicitor will charge you. Be aware that you are ultimately responsible for your solicitor's bill so this means that you may be left paying the difference between this sum and any court order.

However, the court does have the freedom to make the cost order as it sees fit. It is a fundamental part of recent reforms by Lord Woolf (the current Lord Chief Justice) of the civil justice system that the judiciary has greater powers to keep costs reasonable. In particular, the court will consider the conduct of the winning side. For example, the winning party may be penalised if he has been unco-operative; if the value of a claim has been exaggerated; if no reasonable attempt has been made to settle where appropriate or a case has been pursued unreasonably.

■ Ongoing costs

The court can make an order as to costs at any stage in the proceedings and, in particular, during interim applications (i.e. a separate self-contained application made during the course of a case).

■ Different types of hearing

The court will decide what kind of hearing your case will receive (or what kind of 'track' your case will be allocated to). This will have different cost implications. If you make a claim and it is disputed, you will be sent a copy of the defendant's defence and an allocation questionnaire. On the basis of this information a decision will be made as to the most suitable track for your case.

1. **Small claims:** non-personal injury claims that have a financial value of £5,000 or less and personal injury claims with a financial value of £1,000 or less will be allocated to the small claims track. Hearings are informal – see chapter 6. People often represent themselves without a solicitor and legal costs may not be recovered from the other side.

2. **The fast track:** the fast track will be the normal track for any claims that do not come within the small claims track and have a financial value of £15,000 or less. The winning party would expect to recover most of his solicitor's costs from the losing side. Cases are closely managed by the courts: there is a fixed one-day hearing; parties are generally given no more than 30 weeks to prepare and recovered costs are limited. For example, the maximum basic trial costs that may be awarded are £750 for cases where the value of the claim exceeds £10,000, plus an additional £250 if the court considers it necessary for a party's legal representative to be present in addition to an advocate.

3. **The multi-track:** the multi-track is the normal track for all claims for which the small claims and fast track limitations do not apply.

Costs in criminal cases

The general principle of the civil courts – that 'costs follow the event' – does not apply so strictly in the criminal courts. A convicted defendant may not be able to pay because he is destitute or going to prison.

If you are accused of a crime (i.e. if you are the defendant) and the prosecution fails, the courts have the power to award no costs, so you have to pay your own costs; order the prosecuting body (the Crown Prosecution Service or the Department of Social Security) to pay or the government has to pay the costs. As a defendant you should always ask your solicitor to apply for costs because the courts will never award them unless asked.

The magistrates' courts have shown reluctance to award costs. However, the erosion of Legal Aid has meant that they are more likely to award them. On the other hand, the Crown Court (which hears major criminal cases) generally pays costs (unless the defendant was in some way responsible for the prosecution or was acquitted on a technicality).

To get further advice on criminal cases, please refer to page 75.

The retainer

This is simply the agreement (written or oral) made by a solicitor to provide legal advice. It covers the whole relationship between the solicitor and the client. It can also be shorthand for 'retainer fee', meaning the money paid by a client to a solicitor to secure his services.

Money up front

It is entirely normal for a solicitor to ask for money on account at the start of a case. In contentious matters, a solicitor may ask you to make such a payment for both his own costs and expenses. If you refuse to pay a reasonable sum for costs, a solicitor may be entitled to refuse to act for you. In non-contentious matters, a solicitor is limited to expenses and has no right to require payment for costs without a client's prior agreement.

Any money paid to your solicitor goes into a separate client account. This is to ensure that your money never gets mixed up with your lawyer's money or that of any other client.

Solicitors' professional obligations

The solicitors' professional rule book (*The Guide to the Professional Conduct of Solicitors*) sets down their obligations to you – in particular, Practice Rule 15 (costs information and client care) – which provides a useful consumer checklist to concentrate the mind on the issues that may generally crop up (see Appendix).

The solicitors' watchdog, the Office for the Supervision of Solicitors (OSS), has tough powers to reprimand those lawyers who breach its rules, from scrapping the bill to getting the firm struck off. It is fair to say, however, that serious sanctions are rarely exercised – see chapter 7.

A solicitor must ensure that the cost information is not inaccurate or misleading. Instead, it must be clear, provided at the outset of a case, and confirmed in writing as soon as possible.

A solicitor should always keep his client properly informed throughout the case and updated at regular intervals (according to the Guide 'at least every six months'). The solicitor should also let you know of any changed circumstances which may affect costs, the degree of risk involved or the cost benefit of pursuing the matter. In other words, you should never be surprised as to the likely charges.

For a wider consideration on what to expect from your lawyer, see chapter 7.

A recap

- You will be responsible for paying your solicitor's bill regardless of any costs order against your opponent.
- If the case goes to court and you lose, you may have to pay your opponent's costs as well as your own costs.
- If the case goes to court and you win, the court may not order your opponent to pay some or all of your costs or he may not be able to pay all your costs. If your opponent is on Legal Aid, you may not recover costs. You will be left with the shortfall.

How solicitors charge

There are various methods of funding a case used by solicitors:

- Charging by the hour
- Fixed fees
- NWNF
- Legal Aid/the Community Legal Service (CLS)

This chapter deals with hourly rates and fixed fees. The other methods of funding are dealt with in the following two chapters.

The hourly rate

This is the most common method of charging and two thirds of all cases are charged in this way. The hourly rate reflects the time spent by the solicitor dealing with the matter, for example, in meetings, considering and preparing documents, attending court, instructing counsel and experts, and travelling, as well as correspondence, telephone calls, etc. It may seem hard to understand why a plumber charges you £60 an hour for coming out to fix your boiler whereas a solicitor can charge you twice that rate for answering the phone.

However, you should bear in mind that his fee also covers the costs of running the firm, including salaries, premises, support staff, etc.

Hourly rates vary from high street firms where you can expect to pay somewhere between £80 to £120 an hour for advice on private and commercial work all the way through to £350 an hour for a senior partner in a City firm for extremely expert advice on complex points of commercial law.

The first thing that should be emphasised is that price should not be the ultimate deciding factor – if you are looking for non-routine legal advice then it clearly makes sense to see a specialist and pay accordingly. You should also make an assessment as to the experience and quality of your lawyer, see chapter 1.

Do not expect a universal rate. A short amount of time spent on research can reveal striking discrepancies. Increasingly, the legal profession is following the retail market with large regional firms, like the out of town supermarkets, reducing prices through economies of scale. However, they lack the familiarity and local knowledge of the high street practice.

There will be different rates within a firm according to the experience of fee earners – for example, one firm may charge £75 an hour for legal executives through to £150 for the partners.

Solicitors record the time spent on time sheets and for this purpose time is usually divided up into six-minute units (i.e. this will be the minimum time charged). Standard telephone calls and letters are generally entered as one unit each. So if your lawyer's hourly rate is £120, each time you ring him to ask how your case is coming along, you will be charged a minimum of £12!

The hourly rate is a flat rate and in addition a firm may invoice for expenses, such as photocopying, overseas phone calls and fax services. But do also consider that you may be paying barristers' fees if the case

Average hourly rates (£/hr) for partners by work type and by region

	North	Midlands/Wales	London	South	All firms
			£/hr		
Equity partners					
Commercial property	121	120	161	124	130
Probate, Wills and trusts	117	116	143	116	121
Personal injury	124	122	149	127	128
Family law	115	114	140	119	120
Salaried partners					
Commercial property	128	129	187	136	145
Probate, Wills and trusts	119	117	168	129	133
Personal injury	119	124	157	130	131
Family law	114	112	149	124	124

[source: *Law Society's 2001 Business Study*]

Average hourly rates (£/hr) for assistant solicitors by work type

	Single solicitor	2-5 sols.	6-12 sols.	13-40 sols.	41-170 sols.	All firms
			£/hr			
Associate/assistant solicitors						
Commercial property	n/a	104	115	127	141	116
Probate, Wills and trusts	n/a	97	112	119	132	109
Personal injury	n/a	113	112	117	115	114
Family law	n/a	102	106	110	120	106

[source: *Law Society's 2001 Business Study*]

goes to court or if specialist advice is needed. Charges will be exclusive of VAT.

In smaller transactions, fees are payable at the end of a case. Or in a long-running action, bills may be sent out quarterly if, for example, expenses exceed, or are likely to exceed, a certain sum.

If the matter involves litigation work, do not forget that if you lose you will be liable to pay the other side's costs. These costs can far exceed the costs you will pay your own lawyers.

Care and conduct

A solicitor may include an uplift on your bill – this is a percentage increase (e.g. 50 per cent) generally charged to reflect the complexity of a particular case. Law firms traditionally split their fee in two: one figure would represent the strict cost to the firm and the other covers 'care and conduct' and is calculated as a percentage of the first figure. This second sum reflects the profit to the firm for conducting your work (as no profit is made from the first 50 per cent).

The uplift may not be separately listed on your bill. This can be confusing given that it can potentially inflate costs by 100 per cent. In recent years solicitors have been encouraged to ditch the uplift and incorporate it into a flat hourly rate. The reason for this is that many clients thought that they were being charged twice and they did not understand the concept. So it is more common now to be charged £150 an hour, as opposed to £100 plus 50 per cent.

Overcharging

When a solicitor is working on an hourly rate there is always a danger of being overcharged. Or, indeed, of being charged for non-existent hours. One dramatic example of this was a London solicitor who was struck off in 2000 after overcharging a client by approximately £900,000. His client's action against *The Sunday Times* was settled for

£12,000. The newspaper had agreed to pay the reasonable costs of the action later assessed at £128,000. The solicitor's bill, though, was for more than £1 million. When the court came to decide which costs were reasonable, it found the solicitor included a large number of fictional invoices and correspondence.

There are other common (but usually unsubstantiated) horror stories of clients being charged for trainee solicitors reading their file notes on the tube or lawyers racking up the costs of, for example, takeaway pizzas to their clients. Certainly, there is a deeply unhealthy pressure on lawyers within the modern law firm to bill as many hours as possible. One example was an internal memo leaked by disgruntled members of staff at a world famous law firm based in the city of London which suggested a huge pressure to inflate chargeable hours.

This memo (which mainly related to the firm's US practice) revealed that lawyers had a target of 2,400 hours to bill a year in order to get a bonus – this works out at 50 hours a week of billed time on top of the time lawyers were expected to spend on administration and other non-essential activities, such as lunch breaks.

Fixed fees

This form of payment has the obvious appeal of limiting your liability for legal costs and, after the hourly rate, it's the next most common way of charging. The obvious downside is that if your case concludes quickly, then you will end up paying more than you may have on the hourly rate basis. So there is a balance to be struck between the peace of mind of the fixed fee and the assurance that the hourly rate brings that you are paying your lawyer for work actually done. A fixed fee will be inappropriate for most cases which go to court for the obvious reason that litigation can be a very unpredictable (not to mention expensive) venture.

Such arrangements are often used when a solicitor has a good idea of the amount of work involved in a case, which tends to be straightforward non-contentious matters, such as conveyancing, debt collection and drafting jobs such as Wills and tenancy agreements.

However, the more innovative law firms are increasingly using these arrangements in other more complex matters from taking a case to an employment tribunal to commercial work. Some lawyers have cottoned on to the fact that a client will be happy with the certainty of a fixed fee and happy to pay more than he may do for an hourly rate because of that security. One consideration to bear in mind is that a fixed fee inevitably provides an incentive for a lawyer to settle a case as quickly as possible.

Ten tips to keep costs down

1. Do your homework before taking legal advice from a lawyer and you should be able to establish whether you have a legal claim at all. You will also be better able to understand your solicitor.

2. Make sure you have a first free meeting to determine whether you have a claim, either over the phone or in the office.

3. Put your papers in order before handing them over. If you make sure that all your correspondence and other documentation is in chronological order, then you won't end up paying your lawyer for doing it.

4. Ask for an estimate. You cannot hold your lawyer to an estimate but his bill should be reasonable and an estimate can be a guide.

5. Set a legal budget with your lawyer. If you cannot agree one figure, then come up with a range of budgets for the elements of the case. If the work is not appropriate for a fixed fee and the solicitor is going to charge by the hour, you can always agree a ceiling beyond which he cannot go without your express permission.

6. Consider periodical statements of expense, if appropriate, on a monthly basis. This will spread the cost out for you and ensure that you are not presented with a large bill at the end of the case.

7. Confirm instructions in writing. Lawyers are supposed to tell you in advance about the possible level of charges and how the costs are to be calculated. To avoid any problems later on in a case, ask for the information to be provided in writing. Under Law Society rules, solicitors are required to give the best possible information about the likely level of charges.

8. Read your client care letter. All lawyers are obliged to send a client care letter, giving information about their proposed charges, the name and status of the fee earner and details of the person with whom you can raise concerns. Make sure it tallies with what you have previously discussed. For example, if your solicitor has agreed not to exceed £500 without letting you know, then insist that it is mentioned in the letter. If not, write back and say that your instructions are conditional upon it.

9. Pay attention to your solicitor's advice. If he considers the case to be not worth pursuing, think carefully before continuing.

10. Always be courteous and polite to your solicitor and his staff. Do not bother your solicitor with unnecessary phone calls. If he is charging by the hour, you pay for those calls!

For more information about solicitor's charges and, in particular, what to do if things go wrong, see chapter 7.

Chapter 3
Legal Aid

Are you eligible?

What is Legal Aid (CLS Funding)?

If you need to see a solicitor but you cannot afford to pay him, then you may be entitled to support from the Community Legal Service (CLS). What used to be called 'Legal Aid' does not formally exist any more since the system of public funding for all cases was radically overhauled in 2000. It is now officially known as 'CLS Funding', although it is still commonly called Legal Aid. The government provides money to help pay for cases through the CLS fund, which oversees advice and legal representation for people involved in civil cases, or the Criminal Defence Service for criminal cases. Both are administered by the Legal Services Commission (LSC) (formerly known as the Legal Aid Board).

Who is entitled?

You have to show that you cannot pay for your case (i.e. that you are financially eligible) and that you have a sufficiently strong case that you are likely to win. Even if you are working, own your home and have savings, you may still qualify. However, you may well have to pay a contribution towards the cost of taking your case to court.

Will you be financially eligible?

There are strict limits on both income and capital. For example, to receive financial support for initial help, such as drafting a legal letter or obtaining a barrister's opinion, your disposable income (i.e. what you earn minus Income Tax, National Insurance plus an allowance for dependants) must be no more than £621 a month and your disposable capital must be £3,000 or less. If you are going to trial and want financial help, the criteria are different. Your disposable income for most higher levels of claim must be below £707 a month and your disposable capital must not exceed £8,000. For very expensive cases you may still qualify if your capital is above this limit. There are special cases regarding children where you may qualify regardless of finances.

What costs may you face?

If you are better off, you may be asked to pay part of the costs. If you are successful, you may be asked to put some or all of the money or property you recover or keep hold of towards your solicitor's bill if your opponent is not ordered to pay it. This is called the 'statutory charge' and, where this applies, CLS Funding acts as a loan.

What areas of law are covered?

You may be able to get support if your problem is to do with divorce and family; housing (e.g. rent or mortgage arrears, repairs and eviction); welfare benefits; consumer matters (credit, debt and buying goods); immigration; employment; mental health; actions against the police and clinical negligence. As said before, routine personal injury cases have been taken out of the scheme and are now dealt with by conditional fee arrangements, see chapter 4.

What ever happened to Legal Aid?

Strictly speaking, the phrase 'Legal Aid' no longer exists. On its 50th anniversary, New Labour radically overhauled the old system of Legal Aid and struck the phrase from the official lexicon, preferring instead 'CLS Funding'.

As a consequence, now the state's guarantee of legal advice (for those financially eligible and with a good case) no longer exists, except for those accused of criminal offences. However, that's not to say that you will not receive financial help from the state (see page 65 onwards).

For many years, Legal Aid had been in urgent need of reform. 'A society which rations its health service should not object to rationing civil justice,' declared one broadsheet leader in 1999. Certainly not one as wasteful as ours, it went on to argue. At the end of the millennium the Legal Aid budget was perceived to be something of a national disgrace, having topped the £1.6 billion mark and having doubled in that decade alone.

According to the critics, if one case summed up the perceived excesses of the old regime it was perhaps a boundary dispute over a narrow ribbon of land in deepest Staffordshire. On paper, the dispute seemed a rather pointless wrangle over a virtually worthless six-foot-wide strip of land. In the hands of the lawyers, it dragged on for over a decade, and went all the way to the House of Lords taxing the brains of 11 senior judges en route and costing the taxpayer £100,000. Another oft-cited case of totally unmerited excess was a massive legal action involving 13,000 former tranquilliser or sleeping pill addicts. It ran up a bill for £40 million without even making it to the courtroom door.

Critics may just have tolerated the cost of Legal Aid if it was the high price for ensuring equality before the law. But it was becoming clear that this was not the case. In fact, Legal Aid, through the creeping financial eligibility criteria, had become something of a poverty benefit available only to those who were on the breadline. At the time that the Access to Justice Bill was going through Parliament, anyone with a disposable income of more than £61 a week was denied state funded legal advice.

The inept old system appeared to filter out deserving cases and let through the unworthy. It was certainly hard to justify the £4 million taxpayers paid to the millionaire Jawad Hussein, a former adviser to Saddam Hussein, to contest a £33 million embezzlement action. His vast wealth did not preclude him from Legal Aid status, because his six homes dotted around the world were amongst the disputed assets and so were not included.

At the same time, one newspaper contrasted Mr Hussein's case with the desperate plight of Ivan Jones, a 49-year-old paraplegic living on benefits of £187 a week with his wife, who was told that he was too well off for Legal Aid to sue the ex-employers he blamed for confining him to life in a wheelchair. The Legal Aid gravy train, as the editorial writers might have put it, had to come to an end.

The phrase 'CLS Funding' is a misleading but revealing change in terminology because you would not automatically associate it with advice from a lawyer. It is a distinction that reflects a reluctance on the part of government ministers to encourage people to seek redress automatically through the courts. But it also hints at a new way of looking at legal advice. It suggests that help does not necessarily have to come from lawyers but can come from Citizens Advice Bureaux (CABs), law centres and other advice agencies which have been given a more prominent role under the umbrella of the new CLS. There is also a greater emphasis on non-lawyer solutions, such as mediation and arbitration.

The reforms are much more than a rebranding exercise. When introduced, critics attacked the new system of legal funding as having been as much influenced by the bean counters at the Treasury as the policy-makers in the then Lord Chancellor's Department. Controversially, the government has introduced a fixed cap on its budget with unlimited priority for the criminal work and what is left over available for civil work. (The logic for this arrangement is that it would be in breach of the European Convention on Human Rights to deny someone legal advice on a criminal charge and therefore this fund has to be ring-fenced.)

Financial control is central to the new system and the legislation shifts responsibility away from Parliament to government. The rules as to which cases should be funded are now set out in the new Funding Code, replacing the old 'merits test'. It is far easier for the Lord Chancellor to alter the criteria of the code than it ever was to change the merits test, which required the amendment of an Act of Parliament.

The legislation has also introduced a new system of exclusive contracts with the CLS which means that it is no longer possible for any solicitor to advise a client on his problems at public expense, but only those firms or other advice agencies with contracts. In addition, the contracting regime now acts as a quality assurance scheme and a Quality Mark (as shown on page 34) is awarded to all those organisations with contracts or those that meet specific quality criteria.

Huge swathes of civil legal advice have been removed from the system, including routine personal injury work and boundary disputes, which have in theory been replaced by private arrangements run through conditional fee agreements (CFAs) (see chapter 4). The CLS is more tightly focused on social welfare cases, such as immigration, employment and cases involving benefits.

Introducing the reforms, the then Lord Chancellor, Lord Irvine of Lairg, expressed that his aim was to introduce a legal system that 'operates in the best interests of the whole community, not just the financial interests of the legal profession'.

Whilst it is still not unheard of for top QCs to make more than £500,000 a year from Legal Aid, many solicitors on the high street have been struggling to survive on legal rates. Since the introduction of contracting, such problems have been developing into something of a crisis in the legal profession. A recent Law Society survey of 270 firms found that some 78 per cent intended to drop or reduce publicly funded work in the next five years, and one in five were set to leave the field entirely.

The problems in the legal profession are becoming an increasing issue for the consumer looking for access to justice. There is plenty of anecdotal evidence about the difficulties people have finding publicly funded legal advice – not only do you have to be eligible for CLS Funding but you have to find a lawyer who is willing to represent you on this basis.

One newspaper revealed the efforts that one woman in Essex had to go through to find a solicitor to advise her on the financial aspects

Five steps to CLS Funding

Step one

Contact your lawyer or adviser and arrange an appointment to discuss your situation. Take with you all the information you can about your case so that he can give you detailed advice. Write down any questions you may want to ask beforehand.

Step two

Take with you details of both your own and your partner's income – savings and outgoings, recent wage slips, mortgage or rent information, Council Tax payments and bank statements.

Step three

If you are on Income Support or Income-Based Jobseeker's Allowance, bring proof that you are in receipt of these, such as a benefit book.

Step four

If you qualify, the cost of your meeting with the lawyer/adviser will be paid by the CLS fund. You may have to repay these costs if you win. Make sure this is explained to you before you go any further.

Step five

One meeting may be all you need. If your case is more complicated, you may be advised by your lawyer or adviser to take it further and apply for higher levels of CLS Funding. He will explain how to go about this.

of her divorce. 'I called over 20 central London solicitors, all of whose numbers were given to me by the Law Society, only to find after a dismal day on the phone that not one of them took legally aided standard divorce any more,' she said.

Access to decent family law advice has been a problem for a while and it is compounded by the fact that most problems require separate legal advisers for both sides. Citizens Advice research, published in September 2003, revealed other 'Legal Aid advice deserts'. For example, it found that there were no Legal Aid solicitors in the town of Leatherhead, Surrey, and in the whole of Kent there were no housing solicitors offering Legal Aid.

In an effort to honour its public duty to make sure people have access to legal services, the LSC decided last year to plug the gaps in housing advice with a telephone service through a call centre. However, it is worth remembering that the LSC is under a public duty to provide access to legal advice, so if you cannot find help, contact them.

How do you find a solicitor or legal adviser?

For general tips about how to find the right solicitor or legal adviser for the job, see chapter 1. As mentioned on page 34, only organisations with a contract with the LSC can provide advice, so if you already have a solicitor, find out if he has a contract. If not, you can go to a CAB, a law centre or advice centre.

Alternatively, you can have a look in the Law Society Directory of Solicitors and Barristers in your local library or the Yellow Pages and the CLS Directory.

You can also try the CLS Directory telephone service on 0845 608 1122 (minicom: 0845 609 6677) or look on their website www.justask.org.uk.

If you want to talk through a problem, the CLS advise that you approach a 'CLS general help point' – by this they mean a CAB where you can receive advice on, for example, writing a letter, filling in a form or finding out more about any potential claim. 'Specialist help points', such as law centres and solicitors, can offer help with problems relating to, amongst other matters, clinical negligence, immigration, housing or family problems.

When you find a solicitor or legal adviser, it is important that what you tell him about your finances (and your case) is accurate. There are penalties for deliberate false statements and you may have your funding taken away. You must immediately tell him if your finances change.

Advice on civil cases

Note: all figures in this chapter are based on the LSC's own figures as accurate in April 2003. Leaflets about LSC funding and other general legal information leaflets are available from www.legalservices.gov.uk or 0845 300 0343.

There are a number of different, self-explanatory levels of service for civil cases and, as will be seen below, family law advice is treated separately from other areas of civil advice.

- **Legal Help:** provides initial advice and assistance with any legal problem (under the 'old' Legal Aid system, this was known as the Green Form scheme).

- **Help at Court:** allows for someone to speak on your behalf at certain court hearings, without formally acting for you in the whole proceedings.

- **Legal Representation:** provides legal representation in court if you are taking or defending court proceedings (previously called 'civil Legal Aid'). It is available in two forms: Investigative Help where funding is limited to investigating the strength of a claim and Full

Representation where funding is provided to represent you in legal proceedings.

■ **Support Funding:** allows for partial funding of very expensive cases, which are otherwise funded privately, under a CFA (see chapter 4). It is available both for the investigation of the strength of a claim with a view to a CFA and for partial funding of high cost proceedings under a CFA.

Legal Help and Help at Court

■ **What do the schemes cover?**

Legal Help covers general advice, letter writing, negotiating, obtaining a barrister's opinion and preparing written cases if you have to go before a court or tribunal.

Help at Court means that a solicitor or adviser can appear in court on your behalf at a particular hearing, without formally acting for you in the whole proceedings. These schemes enable help from an adviser until charges reach a total of £500 (higher for immigration and asylum cases). Beyond that, the LSC's authority is needed.

■ **Do you qualify?**

You must be able to show that your capital and your income are within the financial limits. The maximum capital you are presently allowed is £3,000. If you are married or living as a couple, your partner's capital and income will be included (except if you live apart or you are seeking a divorce). If you are receiving Income Support or Jobseeker's Allowance, you will be eligible on income. If you are not, the maximum gross income (i.e. total earnings before tax and other deductions) is £2,288 in the past month and, if you fall within that bracket, your disposable income must be below £621. A higher limit applies if you have more than four dependant children in your family.

The statutory charge

Where you gain or keep money or property with the help of CLS Funding, you may have to repay all or some of your legal costs out of that property. In this way, funding can act as a loan. The money or property you get with the help of CLS Funding will first be used to repay your legal costs to the LSC and then you will receive anything left over. For example, if you recovered £10,000 and the cost of your case was £2,000, you would be left with £8,000. Your solicitor cannot pay money out to you until the statutory charge has been dealt with. Normally, it has to be paid as soon as the money or property comes through from the other side. If you recover a home, it may be possible to delay payment of the charge and it will be registered on the house (like a mortgage).

The statutory charge does not apply:

- if you do not gain or keep the money or property that was in dispute;
- if you recover all of your costs from the other side;
- if it is regarding maintenance payments;
- if it is to the first £2,500 or £3,000 of any money/property you gain or keep in divorce cases and most other family proceedings; or
- in Family Mediation and where advice is given under the Help with Mediation scheme, or where advice only is given under the Legal Help scheme, other than family or personal injury after 1 April 2000.

Your solicitor also has limited powers to waive the statutory charge in family or personal injury cases where advice has been given under the Legal Help scheme only. You may have to pay a contribution towards your case whilst the case is running. When the statutory charge is calculated, the LSC will give you credit for any contribution you have paid.

■ **Do you pay a contribution?**

No.

■ **What about other costs?**

The statutory charge applies (see page 68).

Legal Representation

■ **What does the scheme cover?**

There are two different forms of Legal Representation: Full Representation and Investigative Help. Full Representation covers all the work needed to take legal proceedings to trial and beyond. It is available in both family and civil cases, but there are different merits criteria and financial criteria for different types of cases. It is not usually available for personal injury cases (other than the more complex clinical negligence work), but it is available for business disputes, boundary disagreements and libel. Investigative Help is limited to the investigation of the strength of a proposed claim where the prospects of success are not clear and the investigation is likely to be expensive.

■ **Do you qualify?**

You must meet the merits criteria relevant to your type of case and qualify financially. In some cases involving children there are no means or merits criteria.

Merits test

The merits criteria incorporate an assessment of your prospects of success and cost benefit, and may apply, for example, where you have reasonable grounds for claiming damages but the amount involved is small enough to be dealt with by the County court as a small claim.

Qualifying financially

In immigration cases the financial eligibility criteria are the same as for Legal Help. Cases before the mental health review tribunal are not subject to a means test. If you are on Income Support or Income-Based Jobseeker's Allowance, you will qualify for funding automatically on income without having to pay a contribution, but you must be able to show that your capital, including savings, is within the current financial limits.

Income – how do you qualify?

If your gross monthly income exceeds £2,288, you will not be eligible for funding. If your gross monthly income is £2,288 or less, your solicitor will then assess your disposable income (income left after tax and other deductions) and if it is £707 or less, you will qualify (except in immigration cases where the upper disposable limit for Legal Representation is £621).

Income – do you pay a contribution?

No, if your disposable income is £267 a month or less. If it is between £268 and £707 a month, you will have to pay towards the cost of your case from your income. Contributions from income are paid on an ongoing basis. For example, if your disposable income is £303 a month, then the monthly contribution would be £10 a month. No contributions are payable from either income or capital in immigration cases.

Capital – how do you qualify?

To qualify before the immigration adjudicator or immigration appeal tribunal, you must have no more than £3,000 in capital. If your disposable capital is £8,000 or less, you will qualify for all other types. With the exception of immigration work, if your disposable capital is more than these limits, you may still be offered funding if your case is likely to be expensive.

Capital – do you have to pay a contribution?

No, if your free capital as assessed is £3,000 or less, or if you are receiving Income Support or Income-Based Jobseeker's Allowance. Otherwise, you will be asked to use all of your disposable capital over £3,000 to fund the case.

■ What about other costs?

If you satisfy the merits criteria and qualify financially, the LSC will issue a certificate if you do not have to pay a contribution or, if you do, send an offer of a certificate. If you accept, you must pay a contribution from your savings straight away and any contribution from income by monthly instalments. A certificate will then be issued and then your solicitor can look at your case.

What costs do you pay if you win?

The statutory charge applies (see page 68).

What costs do you pay if you lose?

The most you will normally have to pay towards your solicitor's or barrister's costs will be any contribution under your certificate.

Support Funding

■ What does the scheme cover?

It applies for partial funding for personal injury cases (not clinical negligence) and some multi-party actions (where a large number of people bring claims of the same type) where you are bringing your case under a CFA but the action is unusually expensive so justifies some assistance from the LSC. There are two types: Investigative Support and Litigation Support.

■ **Investigative Support:** establishes the strength of a proposed claim with a view to proceeding under a CFA. It is only available where the reasonable costs are likely to be exceptionally high where, for example, the experts' reports are likely to exceed £1,000 or the solicitor's fees are likely to exceed £3,000. There is also a requirement that likely damages must exceed £5,000.

■ **Litigation Support:** provides partial funding of high cost litigation already proceeding under a CFA where the reasonable costs of the litigation are exceptionally high (e.g. the experts' reports are likely to exceed £5,000 or the costs of the case excluding disbursements are likely to exceed £15,000). There are also merits criteria except where the claim has a significant wider public interest.

Advice on family cases

■ **Family Mediation:** provides mediation for a family dispute, and includes establishing whether mediation appears suitable or not. (Mediation is an alternative to using lawyers and does not replace legal or other advice. A mediator does not make decisions for you, but helps you and the other party, usually your partner, to reach your own decisions in a neutral environment. See chapter 6.)

■ **Approved Family Help:** allows for help in relation to a family dispute. This includes Legal Help as well as the issuing of proceedings and representation to obtain information from another party or, for example, to obtain a consent order following an agreement of matters in dispute. (The scheme is divided into two forms: Help with Mediation if you are attending Family Mediation and General Family Help if you are not.)

Family Mediation

■ What does the scheme cover?

Mediation of a family dispute for couples and family members, including disputes relating to children, money and property.

■ Do you qualify?

If you are receiving Income Support or Income-Based Jobseeker's Allowance, you will be eligible on income and capital. In all other cases you must be able to show that your capital and your income are within the current financial limits (including a partner's capital and income unless the relationship is over). The maximum disposable capital is £8,000.

If your gross income exceeds £2,288 a month you will not be eligible. If you are within that bracket, your mediator will assess your disposable income. You qualify if your disposable income is £707 a month or less and your disposable capital is £8,000 or less. A higher income limit applies if you have more than four dependant children.

■ Do you pay a contribution?

No.

■ What about other costs?

The statutory charge will not apply, and you will not be liable to pay any of your mediator's costs.

Approved Family Help – Help with Mediation and General Family Help

■ What does the scheme cover?

It provides help in family cases short of legal representation in contested proceedings. This takes two forms: Help with Mediation which is limited to giving advice to you to support Family Mediation, or General Family Help which covers negotiations where no mediation is in progress. Both levels of service can cover obtaining a court order to confirming any agreement where appropriate.

Help with Mediation enables people to get help from a legal adviser until their costs reach £150 where mediation relates to children issues only, £250 for financial issues only and £350 where mediation covers issues relating to children and finances together.

General Family Help includes representation in proceedings where it is necessary to obtain disclosure of information (e.g. about finances) from another party. It enables people who qualify to get help from a solicitor or adviser until his charges reach an initial limit of £1,500.

■ Do you qualify?

Help with Mediation: if you received funding for your Family Mediation you will automatically qualify. Otherwise, your solicitor will assess your eligibility in accordance with the financial eligibility rules for Family Mediation.

General Family Help: the same rules apply as for Legal Representation.

■ Do you pay a contribution?

Not for Help with Mediation. As for General Family Help, the conditions are the same as those that apply to Legal Representation.

■ What about other costs?

If Help with Mediation is the only level of service given, then the statutory charge will not apply but if General Family Help is given, then the statutory charge may apply.

Advice on criminal cases

The Criminal Defence Service (CDS), administered by the LSC, replaced the old system of criminal Legal Aid on 2 April 2001. In the same way as the CLS, solicitors must hold a contract to carry out criminal defence work funded by the Commission. Alternatively, the Commission directly employs a small number of criminal defence lawyers, known as 'public defenders'. The Public Defender Service provides the following services in exactly the same way as private practice lawyers. Those seeking criminal Legal Aid are free to choose between them.

There are three levels of service:

- Advice and Assistance;
- Advocacy Assistance; and
- Representation for criminal offences.

In addition, duty solicitors are available to offer free legal advice at police stations and magistrates' courts. If the police question you about an offence – whether or not you have been arrested – you have a right to free legal advice from a contracted solicitor. The questioning may be at the police station or elsewhere. There is no means test for such advice. Ask the police to contact the duty solicitor (available 24 hours a day) or your own solicitor. Alternatively, you can choose a solicitor from the list the police keep.

Advice and Assistance

■ What does the scheme cover?

It includes general advice, writing letters, negotiating, obtaining a barrister's opinion and preparing a written case. It enables people of small or moderate means to get help from a solicitor. It does not cover representation in court.

■ Do you qualify?

Capital and income must be within the current financial limits (including your partner's capital and income).

Capital – do you qualify?

If your disposable capital exceeds £1,000, you will not be eligible. This figure includes the value of your savings and anything you own of substantial value, such as jewellery. Houses are not included unless there is more than £100,000 equity after allowing a maximum of £100,000 for a mortgage. Allowances for dependants are deducted from the amount, for example, £335 if you have one dependant (such as a partner). What is left after making these deductions is your disposable capital.

Income – do you qualify?

If you are receiving Income Support, Income-Based Jobseeker's Allowance, Working Tax Credit plus Child Tax Credit(*), or Working Tax Credit with a disability element(*), you will be eligible, unless your disposable capital exceeds £1,000. (*Gross income must not exceed £14,213.)

Disposable income must be £91 a week or less. If you are not receiving one of the above benefits, your solicitor will take the actual income in the past seven days of yourself and your partner and deduct the following: Income Tax, National Insurance contributions, as well as allowances for partners, maintenance (if separated), children and other expenses. What is left after making these deductions is your disposable income.

■ Do you pay a contribution?

No.

Advocacy Assistance

■ What does the scheme cover?

The cost of a solicitor preparing your case and initial representation in proceedings in both the magistrates' court and the Crown Court. It also covers representation for prisoners facing disciplinary charges and cases referred to the Parole Board. It also covers representation for those who have failed to pay a fine or obey a court order of the magistrates' court and are at risk of imprisonment.

■ Do you qualify?

There is no financial test except in relation to prisoners. For this class of work the income limit is £192 a week. The capital limit is £3,000 with allowances for dependants. Income and capital will be assessed in the same way as Advice and Assistance, except that if you receive either Income Support or Income-Based Jobseeker's Allowance, you will automatically qualify on capital.

■ Do you pay a contribution?

No.

Representation

■ What does the scheme cover?

If you have been charged with a criminal offence you can apply for Representation. It covers the cost of a solicitor to prepare your defence before you go to court and to represent you there, including dealing with issues such as bail. It can also cover advice on appeal.

■ Do you qualify?

The court will grant you Representation if it decides it is in the 'interests of justice' that you should be represented based on the information you give in your application form. For example, your case is so serious that if you are found guilty you are likely to go to prison or lose your job, or where there are important questions of law. If the court has decided to refuse Representation because it is not in the interests of justice, you may make another application to the court to review your case.

■ Do you pay a contribution?

You may be asked to pay a contribution if you have been represented in any court other than a magistrates' court. The judge will only ask you to pay a contribution if it is reasonable in all the circumstances of the case, including your means.

■ What is the Duty Solicitor Scheme?

If you have to go to the magistrates' court on a criminal case and do not have your own solicitor, there will usually be a duty solicitor either at the court or on call to give you free advice and representation on your first appearance. There is no means test. Ask the court staff for the duty solicitor. It is best, if possible, to get advice before you go to court.

Advice at the police station

■ Can you get legal advice at the police station?

Yes. Everyone can get Advice and Assistance if they are questioned by the police, whether they have been arrested or not. Even if you tell the police you do not want to see a solicitor, you can change your mind at any time.

■ Will it be free?

Yes.

■ How can you get legal advice?

You can ask the police to contact your own solicitor for you or one you have heard of. If you want, you can ask the police for a list of local solicitors. Alternatively, you can ask the police to contact the duty solicitor who is available 24 hours a day. They are both independent and not employed by the police.

■ Can the police question you without a lawyer present?

Once you have asked for legal advice, generally the police must not question you and you need not answer any questions until you have spoken to a solicitor.

■ Can the police make you wait for legal advice?

Only in some serious cases, and then only if a senior officer agrees. The longest you can be made to wait before speaking to a solicitor is 36 hours after arriving at the police station (48 hours in cases of suspected terrorism).

If you are being sued by someone on Legal Aid

You can make a representation

This is an objection to the granting of CLS Funding. There are two grounds for such an objection: the merits of the case itself (i.e. the case should not be pursued with public money) or the means of the person (i.e. that he has too much money).

How do you make a representation as to the merits of an action?

You should bear in mind the following:

- There should be new information to consider.
- There should be enough time before the trial to investigate the representation (and certainly more than two weeks before the trial date unless there are exceptional circumstances).
- It should relate to something other than a question of fact (which should be left for the court to decide).
- The case should be ongoing.

How do you make a representation as to the means of a person receiving CLS Funding?

You should consider the following:

- It must be about assets that are taken into account in the means assessment (and not, for example, an ordinary motor vehicle of low value).
- It should not be about something that, even if proved true, would not affect the person's financial entitlement.
- It is not about an observation of some part of the person's lifestyle which he could still afford if he was financially eligible for CLS Funding, for example, he has been on holiday.

Chapter 4
No win, no fee
Conditional fees and contingency fees explained

What does 'no win, no fee' mean?

'No win, no fee' (NWNF) is a deceptively simple expression. On one level – and as the name implies – solicitors are paid nothing for their work if they lose, but it also covers agreements whereby solicitors can charge more if they are successful. Until very recently the legal profession did not allow solicitors to have any financial stake in the outcome of a case and as a consequence the arrangements surrounding NWNF are heavily regulated and technical.

But (put simply) there are two types of NWNF:

■ Conditional fee agreements

This is the only type of NWNF that is allowed for the vast majority of cases (with the exception of family and crime). It is the only form of NWNF available for litigation (see note on page 84 for further information). It has two important features:

The success fee

The solicitor is allowed to charge a sum to reward his risk-taking in the event of a successful result which can be as much as double his fees. If you win, the losing side will (generally speaking) pick up this cost.

After-the-event insurance

The general principle of the UK courts is that 'the loser pays'. And so you will not have to pay your own solicitor's costs win or lose, but you could be liable for your opponent's costs. For the price of an insurance premium, you can take out insurance cover, to cover this risk and (in many cases) other outgoings (such as court fees, medical reports or police reports).

■ Contingency arrangements

This is far more straightforward. The solicitor takes as his fee a straight percentage of the award (by contrast with a CFA where the lawyer charges a percentage increase on his fees). It is limited to non-contentious actions (i.e. those not involving court proceedings), and is especially popular in employment tribunals, which are considered for these purposes not to be litigation, as well as Motor Insurers' Bureau claims.

Note: 'no win, no fee' is a colloquialism that does not exactly equate to CFAs. A CFA can also be a discounted CFA where there is 'no win, low fee', i.e. a solicitor charges half the hourly rate to be increased to the full rate plus an uplift if he wins. This arrangement is more common for commercial cases.

Conditional fee agreements

It was only a few years ago that the legal profession frowned upon the very idea of its practitioners having a financial interest in the success of a case in the courtroom. The traditional view was that lawyers should be faithful and impartial servants of the court and any performance-related arrangements (generically known as 'contingency fees') would represent a conflict of interest. In fact, up until 1967, if a lawyer was to take a slice of the spoils it was a criminal offence (known as 'champerty').

Another reason for outlawing NWNF, and one that was no doubt just as persuasive as far as the policy-makers were concerned, was a fear of letting the litigation genie out of the bottle. One cause for the rampant compensation culture in the United States is that their lawyers routinely take as much as 40 per cent of their clients' awards in compensation cases.

Despite these regulations, in certain areas outside of contentious work, it has long been possible for a lawyer to charge contingency fees as long as there is no possibility of court proceedings, for example, where a lawyer is acting for a business acquiring a new property. There are also some less obvious exceptions such as employment tribunals and cases before the Criminal Injuries Compensation Scheme where NWNF has proved popular. It's not at all clear why these tribunals are treated differently from normal courts but lawyers have been quick to take advantage of using such deals in these areas.

Apart from these limited exceptions, the government took its first brave step into the world of NWNF with the introduction of their own heavily regulated version known as CFAs in 1995. This relaxation in the lawyers' rules was a measured response to successive Legal Aid cuts that were effectively freezing out people on moderate incomes from state funding. Conditional fees would enable huge swathes of middle-income people, not eligible for Legal Aid and not able to afford £150 an hour for a lawyer, to have their access to justice – at least that was the idea. The first model allowed lawyers to double their normal fee if a case was successful to reward them for taking on the risk. This meant that you would still be exposed to the other side's legal costs if you lost but you could take out an insurance policy to cover those costs. This new funding method was limited to three discrete areas – personal injury, insolvency and cases before the European Court of Human Rights.

Three years later, CFAs were rolled out to all areas of civil law with the exception of family law. It would seem in poor taste to conduct a NWNF action in a child access or a divorce case – what outcome would you consider to be 'a win'? Intriguingly, ministers have deliberately left the door open for CFAs even in this area.

In this original model there was an inbuilt disincentive for clients because if they won, they lost a significant chunk of their damages in the form of the lawyer's increased fee. And if they lost, they had to pay the winner's costs and, of course, there were no damages.

Access to Justice

New Labour dramatically overhauled the model with its Access to Justice Act. It aimed to solve the problems of the original CFA model by allowing for the recovery of the insurance premium plus the reward for the lawyer's risk-taking from the losing party rather than having the two costs swallowing up the damages.

In a brave move (or a reckless one, depending upon your point of view) the government unleashed this untested model by scrapping Legal Aid in all run-of-the-mill personal injury cases. CFAs were to plug that huge gap left by Legal Aid.

Clearly, the withdrawal of Legal Aid from personal injury was the equivalent of a gun to the head for those lawyers who had to get on with the new regime. But NWNF has also had an enlivening effect in some other areas of the civil law. A good example is in the area of libel where Legal Aid is not available. For example, if a tabloid newspaper mistakenly accused you of some terrible crime or sexual misdemeanour, unless you were very wealthy in the past you suffered in silence. But now the libel courts – once the exclusive preserve of the rich and powerful – have been, to some extent, opened up to normal folk.

However, generally outside personal injury, the legal profession's enthusiasm for NWNF has not been great. Having said that, CFAs have been used in intellectual property disputes (e.g. the young designer whose fashionable T-shirt designs have been ripped off by a well-known high street chain); insolvency (the insolvent businessman who is owed debts but would otherwise have no funds to pursue a legal action); housing disrepair (the tenant who wants to take on the neglectful landlord but has no money) and professional negligence claims (the homebuyer who discovers his new home is riddled with damp which was not picked up by his surveyor). But they also have been used in straightforward commercial cases where, for example, a wealthy businessman is embroiled in a multi-million pound commercial dispute over property ownership. In such a case it may appeal to the client's entrepreneurial spirit that his lawyer takes a share of the risk.

There has been one big limiting factor in the rise of CFAs – the availability of insurance to meet the risk of facing a large bill from the winning opponent.

Enter the claims companies

One legal commentator dubbed the new post-Legal Aid environment 'legal market capitalism'. If the policy-makers had assumed that there would be a neat numerical swap of legally aided cases for CFA cases in personal injury, they were to be proved wrong. They hadn't figured on a new wave of ambitious non-lawyer entrepreneurs in the form of claims management companies entering the personal injury market.

Claims management companies deal with straightforward accident claims – road traffic accidents, slip and trip claims, injuries at work, etc. They come in many forms, from a full claims handling service dealing with all aspects of the case to simple referral schemes that put you in touch with law firms often for no price at all.

The big claims management companies use their marketing might to drum up claims and, if necessary, pass them on to law firms on their panels. There are also claims assessors, non-legally qualified advisers, who take claims for compensation on behalf of people and take a slice of the damages. Both effectively add an extra layer of expense to the process.

It was the new breed of claims companies which ensured that the phrase 'no win, no fee' first entered the language, albeit if it wasn't understood properly. The old Claims Direct led the way with its saturation TV advertising inspired by aggressive US marketing tactics. 'Where there is a blame, there's a claim', was the blunt message of another rival claims giant, The Accident Group (TAG). Both TAG and the old Claims Direct were huge market leaders and they went bust within a year of each other. In the last three years there have been many accident victims who complain that they have seen their damages eaten up by insurance costs. There has also been deep concern from consumer groups about the way some of the claims companies have operated and, in particular, the way they (and their agents) drum up compensation claims.

The old Claims Direct made sizeable inroads into the legal market and at the peak of its powers it represented an unstoppable tidal wave of litigation sweeping up 5,000 new clients every month. But it was to come dramatically unstuck over the recovery of the cost of their insurance premium, which was a whopping £1,250. Their premium had little to do with insurance (only £361 in fact represented insurance costs) and everything to do with paying other costs associated with the claims company model such as its huge marketing campaign and other expenses. The defendant insurance industry unsurprisingly refused to foot the bill and challenged the claims company in the courts. This is still a live issue and accident victims should always try to ensure that their damages are safe by understanding fully that only reasonable insurance costs will be recovered from the defendant insurers.

Their financial problems were compounded by consumer scares. The old Claims Direct went from a hugely successful company all the way to receivership in two years pursued all the way by the media – most notably, Anne Robinson's BBC *Watchdog* programme and *The Sun*'s 'Shames Direct' campaign. The old Claims Direct went bust in 2002; however, a very reputable firm of solicitors Russell Jones & Walker has since bought their name and they plan to operate as the new Claims Direct.

TAG folded in 2003 when its 2,700 staff discovered that they had lost their jobs at its Manchester HQ by text message. As far as consumer critics of claims companies are concerned, there are two abiding stories that spell out the perils of such claims companies. First was the story of Jason (as recounted in the Introduction) who worked in a bar and was scarred for life after having been instructed to empty a tea urn full of boiling water that did not have proper handles. A claims company handled his case and after a two-year wait Jason was left with a cheque for £63 from his total damages worth £1,525. Then there was the story of Lee as featured on the BBC's *Watchdog* programme. A secret camera caught another claims company rep exhorting Lee to put in a bogus claim for a bus crash when he was actually at home. The twin evils of the claims companies as seen by the media and consumer pressure groups are that they left many accident victims penniless and that they have prompted a deluge of worthless claims.

The defendant insurance industry is still fighting what they perceive to be inflated premiums tooth and nail in the courts. Consumer watchdogs continue to raise concerns about hard-sell tactics.

Just to make life more confusing the distinction between claims companies and solicitors' firms is blurring as lawyers have aped the marketing tactics of their rivals. For example, the Law Society endorses one scheme, Accident Line (www.accidentlinedirect.co.uk), which is as good a place as any to start looking for a personal injury lawyer. Law firms are also forming their own collectives (e.g. InjuryLawyers4U – see www.injurylawyers4u.co.uk) to take on the marketing might of the claims companies which exist simply to put a client in contact with a solicitor.

Costs crisis

Challenges over costs by the insurance industry have now become a feature of this post-Legal Aid landscape and have effectively clogged up the legal system. The system ground to a complete halt for several months in 2001 when thousands of cases were held up whilst the Court of Appeal had to rule on the level of insurance premium and reward for risk that it was reasonable to recover from the other side. This ruling (*Callery v Gray*) was absolutely crucial and threatened to leave many accident victims' damages decimated by the insurance costs from their own damages.

More recently another technical legal challenge involving TAG left over 200,000 cases waiting on its outcome. It also threatened the livelihood of 700 law firms who were dependent upon the company for work.

Court challenges keep coming at an alarming regularity. The only conclusion that can be drawn with any certainty is that CFAs, whilst being effective in many cases, are beset by teething problems.

How they work and what you need to know

Conditional fees are a fiendishly complicated way to achieve a very simple effect. Lawyers can be surprisingly poor communicators and the increasing number of intermediaries in the form of claims management companies interposing themselves between the client and lawyer further muddies the waters.

The consequence of this is more often than not that people sign up to what are effectively insurance products without any clear understanding of what they mean. One early study into CFAs revealed that out of 40 clients interviewed, only one understood how his case was funded. More alarmingly, the research also revealed that a number of the lawyers did not fully understand how they worked either!

Sadly, there have been many unhappy stories in the press so far of accident victims left without a penny to their names after costs were deducted from their award of damages. But it is fair to say that nearly all of these cases were personal injury claims and were handled by claims management companies. To avoid the pitfalls, there are some basic issues to resolve.

Is a solicitor responsible for your claim?

If he is, you are dealing with a professional who is qualified, regulated and has insurance. If not, you may be dealing with someone who has little or no training. In that case, if things go wrong, you may have little or no redress against him. So if a solicitor is not responsible for your case, then why not?

For many accident victims the first point of entry into the legal system has not been a solicitor at all, but the representative of a claims management company. Claims companies have their representatives parading up and down high streets and in shopping centres signing up accident victims to their insurance-based products. Most people find their hard-sell antics pretty distasteful, and there is well-documented evidence that reps of at least one of the biggest companies were drumming up not only unworthy but, in some cases, false claims. Typically, they will work on commission with strict weekly targets for the number of claims they have to generate and they can use very aggressive sales techniques. But if you have a legitimate claim, the chances are you do not need to be told by someone else!

■ To avoid any confusion, make sure the person who is responsible for your case is a solicitor.

Is your lawyer paying someone else for your case?

It is against Law Society rules for a solicitor to pay for a case (although there is considerable pressure from the Office of Fair Trading to relax the ban on the grounds that it is anti-competitive). The situation may arise because an unqualified and unregulated claims assessor will attempt to settle your accident claim on a NWNF basis (usually by taking a straight cut of the award). If he cannot settle the case because it is disputed, he will sell the case on to a solicitor who is allowed by law to handle contentious work.

If this is the situation, then it is not a great start as technically your solicitor is breaking his professional body's own rules. Having said that, the practice is reasonably commonplace and ignored by the Law Society. Do bear in mind, however, that the lawyer may be required to act in a certain way – for example, he may get you to sign up to a loan or use a particular after-the-event policy with a premium that he cannot guarantee he will recover.

■ Make sure that your solicitor is independent and able to act solely in your interests.

Are you signing up to a Consumer Credit Agreement?

A CFA is a highly regulated agreement that you must sign but be wary of signing up to anything else. You may well need a loan to cover the insurance premium and any disbursements but, on the other hand, you may not. In most straightforward personal injury cases there should not be a need for such a loan. The usual model for a claims company is that the client must sign a Consumer Credit Agreement first. The idea is that the loan is used to purchase the insurance policy and the sum is recovered by the solicitor as an expense (or 'disbursement' in legal speak) at the end of the case from the losing party and the loan pays for itself.

You will never recover the interest. If the premium is large (£1,500), the annual percentage rate is high (20 per cent), the case long (two years) and your claim relatively small (£2,000), then you will pay a large sum in interest alone (£600).

- Is it really necessary to take out a loan? If so, make sure that the repayment terms and the APR are reasonable.

Does 'no win, no fee' mean 'win, no cost'?

Ask your solicitor whether he will guarantee that your damages will come to you intact. You may be responsible for certain costs, such as an excessive insurance premium, which can effectively wipe out damages. In the case of the old Claims Direct, this has meant that thousands of accident victims have been left penniless.

There is an obscure (and unhelpful) rule called the 'indemnity principle'. It means that solicitors can only claim from the defendant what they have agreed their client would pay. Their problem is that CFAs involve the promise that clients will not pay anything. It effectively prevents lawyers from assuring their clients that they will receive their damages intact even if they are happy to do so. The government has announced plans to scrap the rule. By the time of going to press, there should be no reason why a solicitor cannot make such a promise.

■ Make sure that your damages will be recovered intact.

Do you understand what you are signing?

Since the arrival of NWNF, the average length of the first solicitor-client interview has doubled in length from 30 minutes to an hour and a half. This will give you some idea as to the complexity of CFAs. Remember that a CFA is an insurance product and it is you who will be liable for costs. Make sure you understand what is going on.

■ Don't leave the office until you fully understand what you have signed.

Before you sign on the dotted line...

The basic principles of CFAs are straightforward enough. Here is a checklist to ensure that you avoid the pitfalls:

- Deal directly with a solicitor. Only a solicitor will be legally qualified to handle your case. If things go wrong, he is regulated by the Law Society and is obliged to have professional indemnity insurance.

- Make sure that your lawyer does not pay someone else for your claim. Only an independent lawyer can offer you fully impartial and independent advice.

- Think twice before signing a loan agreement. In most routine cases – certainly in run-of-the-mill personal injury cases – there is no need to take out a loan. Do remember that you will be responsible for all interest payable on a loan.

- Make sure that your damages will be intact. Many firms will provide an assurance that there will be no sums deducted from damages.

- Understand what you sign.

A closer look at the CFA

If you have a clear understanding of your potential liabilities under a CFA as explained previously, then you will avoid the pitfalls. However, the next section looks more closely at the mechanics of these complex arrangements.

An overview

It is important to keep in mind the two different cost consequences that you may face both if you win and if you lose (see chapter 7).

If you lose: a CFA places the risk upon your solicitor, so he will not be paid if the case loses. However, you will still have to pay the defendant's costs. For this reason you can and should take out after-the-event (ATE) insurance to cover those costs.

If you win: the lawyer is entitled to charge for the risk of taking on a case, called the 'success fee'. Most, if not all, of the success fee plus the ATE premium can be recovered from the other side. If those costs are not considered to be 'reasonable' by the court, then these expenses may come out of your damages.

Defendant insurers (who have to foot the bill) have been challenging both success fees and insurance premiums in the courts on a very regular basis. This has led to many accident victims losing their damages. You should be aware of your potential liability before entering into a CFA.

What is the success fee?

It is the reward for a lawyer taking on the risk of the case (sometimes called the 'uplift'). The success fee, which is not linked to the compensation award, is capped at 100 per cent of a lawyer's fees – in other words, he can double his normal fees. As well as the risk, solicitors can charge a subsidy element to compensate a lawyer for not being paid 'on account' (throughout the life of a case), as he would have been under Legal Aid. Many solicitors waive the subsidy part and, unlike the risk element, it is not recoverable from the opponent.

The success fee should reflect the lawyer's view of the chances of success. For example, a simple rear end shunt in a car is no great risk and so it should be fair to charge somewhere in the region of between five and 20 per cent, whereas a complicated commercial action may warrant the 100 per cent uplift.

Success fees should not be a concern for you, because on a 'win' the other side pays. If the court disallows the success fee because it is too high, you will only be responsible if the court says that you should be. If that happens, you will be able to ask the court to have a closer look at your lawyer's bill (a process known as 'an assessment', see chapter 7). But it would be very rare for a lawyer to have his success fee challenged and then insist that his client foots the bill.

- If a subsidy element is to be charged, ask how it is calculated. If it relates to disbursements paid out by your solicitor, consider paying upfront if you have the money in order to reduce costs.

- Ask whether the solicitor's hourly rate is the same as he expects to recover from the other side. Otherwise you may be landed with the shortfall.

What is after-the-event insurance?

ATE insurance is a form of legal expenses insurance (LEI). Unlike other forms of insurance, you are effectively taking out insurance for something that has already happened. You cannot ring up an insurance broker to find out about ATE insurance; instead, you are in the hands of the lawyers who will arrange the cover for you. Insurers often have exclusive deals with solicitors. Of course, if you are not happy with the insurance policy, you are free to find another lawyer. If your case is successful, the other side picks up the cost of the premium.

There are a number of insurers who offer ATE insurance. Policies and costs vary significantly from insurer to insurer, but here are some common features. All policies are designed to pay the other side's costs if you lose. There will be limits to the amount they will pay, so you need to be sure the policy covers all the likely costs. Some policies will also cover out-of-pocket expenses (what the lawyer calls disbursements), such as doctor's fees, court fees and fees for medical records. Some, but not all, policies will cover your own barrister's fees. Some offer 'retrospective' cover to fund costs and disbursements that are already incurred. These are commonly included in clinical negligence claims.

Premiums vary massively and outside the area of personal injury there are no industry norms. At the time of going to print, the price for a modest value personal injury claim may be somewhere between £300 and £400. But even these vary. For example, the now defunct market leader, TAG, was offering a premium that was just shy of £1,000 in 2003. For more complex personal injury claims (such as stress or industrial disease), you can expect to pay anywhere between £1,000 and £8,000 for the same risk.

Outside the area of personal injury, premiums are even less predictable. One insurance broker received three quotes for the same complex risk. The lowest was £700, the middle price was more than twice that and the most expensive was £6,000. As a rule of thumb, one should expect to pay somewhere between 20-30 per cent of the costs liability. The prohibitive price of insurance outside personal injury is the main reason why CFAs have yet to take off elsewhere.

There are also other much less common forms of ATE insurance that a solicitor may use. As an alternative to a CFA, there is 'both sides costs' (BSC) insurance which will pay both your own and your opponent's solicitor's fees and out-of-pocket expenses whether you win or lose. (If you win, you should recover your own solicitor's fees and your disbursements from your opponent, and so you would not need to claim under the insurance.) It is only offered by a small number of insurers and claims management companies. It also tends to be described as NWNF so you should be aware of the difference. BSC policies are more expensive than CFA insurance. However, a BSC policy is not a CFA, so a success fee will not be included. As a result, in some cases this may well be a cheaper option than a CFA premium plus a success fee of up to 100 per cent.

Do you need ATE insurance at all? There are some firms that believe that you don't. There are many cases where the lawyer, or more likely the client, considers his case to be sufficiently strong and as a result does not want to support it with insurance. However, do note that the practice of offering NWNF arrangements without a CFA (called 'speccing', which also covers operating without a valid CFA) is technically illegal. It may also be an indicator of a firm's poor claims record or lack of specialisation.

In practice some firms will offer to indemnify the client against the other side's costs. It is a confident or brave firm (probably both) that does this. It is easy to see why. A firm that uses ATE cover will only be vulnerable to losing its own profit costs but without ATE it will have to pay for its own disbursements plus the defendant's costs. From the client's point of view, such an approach may well be a good thing and it rules out any problems with recoverability. If, however, a firm runs into financial problems, the client may still face liability for costs. Be aware that without a cast iron guarantee, you will be ultimately responsible for costs.

◼ Whatever the agreement, check with your solicitor to see whether he expects to recover the full cost if you lose.

What happens if the other side wants to settle?

When the other party makes you an offer to settle the case out of court (known as 'a Part 36 offer'), and the offer is refused, you run the risk of paying all the costs afterwards if you go to court. The courts are keen for parties to settle, and offer incentives for doing so. An ATE insurer may not be happy to be faced with such a cost and may want you to settle. You need to be clear what you regard as a win and, if at all possible, define it as such in your CFA. For example, the acceptance of a reasonable payment may be regarded as a win. Some policies will protect damages on settlement, others will not, and so it is well worth checking. The key issue is to understand what happens (and what risks there may be) if a case settles out of court.

- You should be clear as to what you consider to be an acceptable outcome if the case settles.

Other expenses

As mentioned before, some insurers ask clients to enter into loan agreements to cover the cost of the insurance premium and out-of-pocket expenses. If you lose, the insurance covers the cost of the premium and if you win it should be received from the other side. However, do remember that you will be responsible for the loan.

If there is no loan, one has to bear in mind the expense of medical reports and other records about you, as well as court fees. Will you be needing a barrister? If counsel is required, solicitors can enter into a NWNF arrangement with barristers in which case you shouldn't have to worry about the expense (counsel will not be paid in an unsuccessful case, and the other side pays on a win). Otherwise their fees are regarded as another expense. The only other time you may have to pay your lawyer's costs is if you did not co-operate with him in the prosecution of your case, or you misled him.

- Find out what other out-of-pocket expenses you may have to pay.

Three examples of CFAs

In this hypothetical example an award for damages is made of £5,000. The court has also made a costs award of £1,750 (although the costs incurred have in fact come to £2,000) plus disbursements (mainly court fees and medical reports) of £500. Note that:

- solicitors are usually entitled to charge a small extra sum to represent the risk of taking on a case (success fee – risk);
- solicitors are also entitled to charge the subsidy element (success fee – subsidy); and
- the solicitor is required to specify in the CFA his hourly rates, the success fee (split between risk and subsidy) and the reasons for the success fee.

So:

- ask whether the solicitor's hourly rate is the same as he expects to recover. Make sure you are not landed with the shortfall;
- if you win and a subsidy element is charged, ask how this is worked out. If this relates partly to disbursements to be paid on your behalf by the solicitor and you have sufficient funds to meet them yourself, consider doing so to reduce costs;
- check the price of the ATE premium and ask whether the solicitor expects to recover it in full if you lose.

Example one

Item	Expenses	Receipts	Balances
Compensation	0	5,000	5,000
Basic costs	2,000	1,750	-250
Success fee – risk	400	400	0
Success fee – subsidy	200	0	-200
Disbursements	500	500	0
ATE premium	350	350	0
Total	3,450	8,000	4,550

Example two

Most solicitors, as a matter of course, charge nothing for the subsidy element of the success fee. They may also voluntarily waive basic costs not recovered from the loser, although they may be reluctant to agree to this formally because of the indemnity principle (see page 92). In the meantime, if your solicitor says that he will charge nothing for the subsidy element of the success and it is his usual practice to waive his basic costs, you can probably believe him. It is a good deal for you as it is 'no win, no cost' and 'win, no cost'.

Item	Expenses	Receipts	Balances
Compensation	0	5,000	5,000
Basic costs	1,750	1,750	0
Success fee – risk	400	400	0
Success fee – subsidy	0	0	0
Disbursements	500	500	0
ATE premium	350	350	0
Total	3,000	8,000	5,000

Example three

This is what happens when a court refuses to allow the full premium to be paid to the winning client. This example features a BSC premium (but it could equally feature ATE insurance).

Item	Expenses	Receipts	Balances
Compensation	0	5,000	5,000
Basic costs	1,750	1,750	0
Success fee – risk	0	0	0
Success fee – subsidy	0	0	0
Disbursements	500	500	0
BSC premium	1,250	350	-900
Interest on premium loan	350	0	-350
Total	3,850	7,600	3,750

As you can see from the three examples – all marketed as NWNF – there are wildly different results on a win.

[source: *David Marshall, senior partner at London firm Anthony Gold and president of the Association of Personal Injury Lawyers*]

What about defendant CFAs?

What happens if you are sued and you want to instruct your lawyer on a NWNF basis? In theory, this is entirely possible and the Access to Justice Act deliberately envisaged this possibility.

Nonetheless, conditional fees remain almost exclusively the preserve of the claimant, but there are the slightest stirrings of interest from pioneering law firms. For example, the troubled supermodel Naomi Campbell recently took on *The Mirror* over revelations about her alleged drug problems. A relatively minor character was Campbell's former PA, Vanessa Frisbee, who was represented on a CFA.

The theoretical problem is what constitutes a 'win' for a defendant but this issue is merely awkward, not insurmountable. Clearly, if you are a small business and are being sued for £10,000 for breach of contract, a good result would be settling out of court for £5,000, which could be regarded as a 100 per cent success, or £7,500 as a 25 per cent success.

However, there doesn't seem much activity here – only in the libel field.

Contingency fees

What is a contingency fee?

In these arrangements, the solicitor receives his fee as a percentage of the award. By contrast, under a CFA, a lawyer is allowed an increase on his fees in the event of a successful result.

Contingency fees are popular for funding employment claims. The employment tribunal represents a somewhat anomalous exception to the ban on contingency fees in litigation. The going rate for the solicitor's fee is a straight 33 per cent cut of an applicant's damages.

Such an arrangement has the virtue of simplicity, certainly when compared to CFAs. Also in the employment tribunal there is no 'loser pays' rule and so, generally, you will not be landed with the other side's costs.

Employment tribunals

Costs are unpredictable when taking an employer to the employment tribunal in, for example, an unfair dismissal case or a sex discrimination case. According to employment law specialists, one can expect to pay in the region of £5,000 just to get a case to tribunal. Costs can then increase in proportion to the length and complexity of a hearing, but are generally between £5,000 and £10,000. However, the majority of cases settle before a hearing.

Despite damages being 'uncapped' (i.e. theoretically limitless) for discrimination cases, the typical award for race discrimination was only £5,263 and £5,000 for sex discrimination in 2001. For unfair dismissal cases, the average award was slightly higher at £5,917.

The great advantage of contingency fees in this context is absolute security – if you lose, you are not going to be saddled with a huge bill. But that security comes at a price. One can expect to pay somewhere between 30 per cent of an award in a straightforward case and as much as half the award for more complex cases. A lawyer will consider the value of a claim (the smaller the likely award, the greater the cut), the prospects of success and its complexity (e.g. the number of documents and witnesses involved).

Whilst the simplicity of contingency fees is appealing, considerable care should be taken before signing up to such an agreement. There can be hidden costs. Here is a checklist of issues to consider:

- Consider other sources of funding. Are you a member of a trade union? Do you have LEI? Will you be eligible for Legal Aid (CLS Funding is not available for representation before a tribunal but Legal Help may be available for the preparation of a case, see chapter 3)?

- Are you dealing with a solicitor? Only a solicitor will be legally qualified, regulated and have professional indemnity insurance. If one law firm does not offer contingency fees, keep looking because many do.

- Make sure that VAT is included. Most lawyers or advisers will include VAT.

- What out-of-pocket expenses are included? The main consideration may be counsel's fees if your adviser does not do his own advocacy, so check if your solicitor is a solicitor-advocate. At any rate, you will have to pay for him to attend the tribunal. If your legal adviser is at one end of the country and a tribunal hearing is at the other, there may be considerable travel and accommodation costs. There are no court fees.

- What happens in the case of an early settlement? A downside of the contingency fee arrangement is that it gives the lawyer an obvious incentive for dealing with a case quickly. There are two problems with this: you want your lawyer to be acting in your best interests and not his own and, second, you may lose out in damages for a case that settles within a couple of weeks. One solution to this problem is to have a fee arrangement that is based on an hourly rate but is capped at one third of the damages.

- Make sure that you do not have to pay the other side's costs. There are a number of circumstances in which a tribunal can order an applicant to pay costs. In 2001, the cap on such orders was raised from £500 to £10,000 to discourage applicants pursuing hopeless cases. In the last decade the number of costs awarded has trebled but it still represents only three per cent of all cases that the tribunals deal with.

Chapter 5

Other sources of legal help

Legal expenses insurance and unions

This chapter features a number of ways of funding legal actions that may be available to you for no extra expense and which are very frequently overlooked. In particular, there is the representation provided by legal expenses insurance (LEI) as well as the legal services offered by trade unions and other membership groups.

According to government figures, there were more than 17 million people in the UK who paid premiums for LEI cover [source: *Modernising Justice* 1998]. It is usually bought as an 'add-on' or simply given away with household or motor insurance. Policies attached to household insurance will usually cover personal injury, consumer claims, tenancy and neighbourhood disputes. Whereas motor policies will cover the cost of compensation for any accident that is not the policyholder's fault. They can represent excellent value for money, as the average cost is less than £20 a year and provides up to £50,000 worth of cover. There is evidence to suggest that many policyholders are unaware that they have purchased such cover in the first place or come to forget about it later, despite the fact that it can provide an incredibly useful service.

There are almost seven million members of trade unions and all offer legal services to members and their families – from basic helplines, full representation in court, to free or cut-price conveyancing and Will writing services. Motoring organisations, such as the RAC, also offer legal services and it is becoming an increasingly important fringe benefit.

Generally speaking, such schemes can be limited in scope but, if they are appropriate, they can be absolutely invaluable. A feature common to both insurance and union schemes is that people who are covered are too often ignorant of the benefits which are available at no extra cost.

What is legal expenses insurance?

It is an insurance policy to provide you with protection against the costs of bringing or defending legal action. In this chapter we are dealing with a form of LEI that is known by lawyers as 'before-the-event' (BTE) insurance (as opposed to no win, no fee (NWNF) insurance which is called 'after-the-event' (ATE) – see chapter 4).

What is the difference between after-the-event and before-the-event insurance?

There are three essential differences between ATE and BTE insurance. ATE insurance covers a specific action that has happened; the policy lasts as long as the legal action; and the premium is considerably more pricey than a BTE policy. (For a straightforward road traffic accident you can expect to pay as much as £200 whereas BTE can be free with your motor insurance and may be less than £20 a year when bought as an add-on with your household policy.)

How does it work?

Most policies are sold in connection with other existing policies or given away as add-ons to motor policies or, to a lesser extent, home insurance policies. But they can also be bought as standalone policies where policyholders pay an annual premium.

What does it cover?

It depends upon the policy but it can cover disputes with employers, problems with neighbours regarding noise and boundary disputes, as well as nightmare holidays. The costs may include solicitors' fees, together with any costs relating to the case (e.g. payments to expert witnesses) and the other side's costs if the case is lost.

Do you have legal expenses insurance?

You may well be covered without realising it and infuriatingly insurers who sell the policies often do little to remind policyholders of the cover and in many cases do not send them copies of the policy. So do some research!

If you have checked your paperwork and you are not covered, you may want to consider buying a standalone policy or paying an extra premium when you renew your existing policies. If you consult a solicitor about pursuing a conditional fee arrangement (see chapter 4), he is obliged to make reasonable efforts to see if you are covered by a BTE policy and, if there is, he is obliged to contact the BTE insurer. It may be possible to keep your original solicitor if you wish to do so – see page 112.

An overview

Under a good scheme you will have access to a lawyer who will establish whether you have a legal claim or not. It will immediately remove most (if not all) of the financial risk of pursuing your rights. It also has a deterrent effect – if people know that you have it, they know that you are able to defend yourself and so are less likely to pursue you through the courts. Having said that, LEI does have its own significant limitations.

LEI is a relatively new form of insurance cover and has only been available in the UK since circa 1975. It can represent great value for money. Typically, it may offer a 24-hour helpline and cover employment and contract disputes, as well as personal injury claims. So it can be more beneficial financially when you take into consideration the expense of solicitors.

The Consumers' Association has long been a fan of LEI and a recent *Which? Magazine* report recommended that if people were not covered through motor or home policies, they should consider taking out such a policy.

Insurance companies have become increasingly keen on LEI over the last few years. There is an argument of self-interest at work here as the insurance industry, which pays for the defendant's legal costs anyway, sees it as a way of controlling costs.

According to the Association of British Insurers, the total premium paid to insurers was £102,307,000 in 1999. Since then the government has sanctioned NWNF arrangements and the insurance industry is now viewing BTE as a safer bet than conditional fees because (they would say) lawyers and claims companies are being paid too much under conditional fee agreements (CFAs). Consequently, insurers have been increasing their interest in the add-on policies of late, such as DAS (probably the biggest name in the market to date) which announced a tie-up with the Halifax and offered one year's free legal protection to all their mortgage-related home insurance customers – in total, to approximately four million people.

But LEI in the UK does not have the prominence that it has on the continent. In Germany, more than 40 per cent of the population has cover and there has been talk of making legal insurance compulsory in Belgium.

It remains to be seen how long LEI policies will represent such a great deal. One reason why such insurance is relatively cheap is because it is massively under-used. No doubt as LEI becomes more successful, the cost of its premiums will increase in proportion with its profile.

Types of policy

Household legal expenses insurance

It is sometimes called 'personal' or 'family protection'. They are much wider in scope than motor LEI and normally cover personal injury, employment and consumer disputes. (Policies tend to cost £10 to £15 a year and provide a maximum pay out of £50,000 for a claim.)

Motor legal expenses insurance

Most motor policies now offer LEI to recover 'uninsured losses'. This refers to money paid out following a car accident where it is not your fault and which is not covered by your policy. Basically, your policy indemnifies you for repairs to your car, which your insurer recovers from the guilty side. However, it will not pay for out-of-pocket expenses. When you are the innocent victim of an accident, the guilty driver's insurer will pay these but not without at least checking and possibly fighting. Uninsured loss recovery provides someone to argue your case for you.

In a small number of cases, the cost is built into the policy and you don't have to pay a thing. Otherwise, LEI is available as an optional add-on (costing between £10 to £15 a year for £50,000 cover). Typically, it will cover everything from the recovery of your policy excess, the costs of hiring an alternative vehicle, plus the compensation payments for injuries and damage to your possessions. You may find that although you buy LEI attached to your car insurance, your LEI insurer is a different company.

Standalone policy

This is a policy that you can buy independently of other insurance arrangements. The insurance industry seems to have shown little enthusiasm for such policies in recent years. At the time of going to press there is one standalone policy on the market, and for an annual subscription of £200 it offers cover of up to £50,000 per claim for the policyholder plus their family members as well as access to a 24-hour helpline. Because it is not attached to any other insurance product, you do not have to worry about losing cover when you change household or motor insurers.

What you need to know

Check for existing cover

It is worth checking that you do not have cover attached to any other policy and it is also worth considering what protection a partner's policy may offer you. Also bear in mind similar services offered by trade unions and other organisations – see page 113.

Read the small print. This is always the obvious advice when signing up to any form of insurance, but it's doubly relevant in this context as, chances are, you will be buying LEI over the phone as part of another bigger policy. As a result, you are unlikely to know what are the right questions to ask and in the past telesales staff have proved reluctant to promote a product that they do not know much about. In reality, little information is passed on to policyholders prior to a purchase – either written or oral. In many cases, policyholders see only the wording after they have signed up to the product.

A report by *Which? Magazine* (April 2001) examined the small print of the policies of seven major companies and found them lacking in a number of serious respects. According to *Which?*, 'Those selling it, usually staff at call centres, do not always mention exclusions and important conditions and they sometimes can't or won't explain the product properly to customers. Another problem is that you sometimes don't get to see a policy booklet until after you've taken out cover.' *Which?* also noted that the wording was particularly incomprehensible – so if you are in doubt, ask.

What are the limits?

There can be strict limits on what is covered by a policy, so check the general exclusions in the policy document. For example, it may not include legal proceedings between family members (such as matrimonial disputes), a libel action or business problems if you work from home. Most policies will also exclude disputes involving building and construction, and grievances that arose before the policy started. Policies claiming to be 'family' policies are quite particular about their definitions of who exactly comprises a family. It may be worth checking whether policies cover partners or adopted or foster children.

How strong is your case?

You should also be aware that both motor and household legal expenses add-ons only cover you for claims that appear to have reasonable prospects of winning. That decision is ultimately down to the insurer. As a broad rule of thumb, if your chances are deemed to be greater than 50-50, you should qualify. Insurers tend to bury this condition in their policies or, in some cases, omit to mention it at all. So beware!

If your claim is turned down, you can argue your case. Some policies will give reasons for the decision. This can be an expensive process as you will have to provide evidence to substantiate a claim but the insurer can refund such a cost if they take the case on. Find out if your insurer will cover your costs in this case.

Watch the clock

There can be a time lag built into a policy before it comes into effect. For example, the period can be as long as six months in the case of a dispute with neighbours. If you are involved in a dispute over a survey on your new property and it was completed before the move and you have since taken out LEI, then the dispute will not be covered. This is also worth bearing in mind if you change your contents insurance when you move house.

Once a likely claim has arisen you should contact your insurer as soon as possible. For example, one insurer specifically excludes any claim reported more than 180 days after the person 'should have known' about the claim.

Who does your solicitor act for?

'I want my own lawyer and not my insurer's.' It is a complaint often made about LEI – in other words, there is a perception that the solicitor's first duty is to the insurer and not you, the client. But this is wrong – your lawyer's professional duty extends only to you, his client.

Can you choose your own solicitor?

Yes. However, there is some debate as to when policyholders can exercise their right to choose a legal representative of their choice. Wording varies and some policies will claim the right to retain their lawyers until proceedings have started. (Industry watchdogs – including the Insurance Ombudsman and Financial Ombudsman Service – and the courts have expressed concern that choice should be restricted in this way.) If you want your solicitor to represent you from the start, then you should ask.

Trade unions, professional bodies and other organisations

Many membership organisations offer differing amounts of free legal advice – from trade unions representing their members in employment disputes and work-related accidents to motoring organisations, such as the RAC, offering a personal injury scheme in the event of a motor accident. More often than not, legal services are included in the price of membership and they are structured in a similar way to LEI.

Clearly, the ability to defend its members in the courts has always been central to the identity of any trade union and over recent years, they have increasingly built up their range of legal services. Even if you don't have a strong belief in trade unionism and solidarity, the employment protection and legal services are good reasons for signing up.

Many unions provide a broadly similar package of legal help for union members and their families in the UK. There are in the region of 18 million people who can avail themselves of free legal help. Many union members are not aware of the services that are provided for free (in exactly the same way as legal expenses policyholders do not know that they are covered). There has been a deep frustration in the union movement over members who have been ripped off by claims companies over personal injury claims when they were covered by their own schemes and should have instructed union lawyers in the first place.

However, unions often deliver a mixed message, for example, they will back motor insurance policies including LEI which simply duplicate their own legal services that are offered as part of the membership.

The Britain's biggest trade union Unison, which has 1.3 million members and represents public sector workers, offers a fairly typical package. It claims to have won more than £350 million in compensation for members involved in work-related personal injuries, such as assaults, industrial diseases and accidents at work. It also covers accidents outside work for its members as well as for the family, such as road traffic accidents, and slip and trip cases. The union also offers members free legal representation if they face criminal charges arising out of their work and for road traffic offences if the member's job is at risk. (Such services are often industry specific, so firefighters may be covered for driving without due care and attention and social workers against accusations of child abuse.) It can also provide advice or represent members who experience immigration problems which threaten their employment.

Outside of the workplace, Unison will offer free legal advice on any matter not related to work by providing a free 30-minute telephone interview with a solicitor as well as a free initial screening service for members who have been affected by medical negligence. A free Wills service and cut-price conveyancing are also available. In order to qualify for legal help, you must have been a member for at least 13 weeks before realising that you needed assistance. Many of the services are extended to members of the family. There are similar packages available for members of other big unions, such as Amicus-AEEU, the Fire Brigades Union and the National Union of Journalists. The schemes are run by Thompsons solicitors who provide legal advice for a total of 64 trade unions.

There are also similar schemes for employers. For example, the Federation of Small Businesses (FSB), which has 180,000 members, provides a 24-hour legal advice helpline covering business and personal legal advice. It specifically covers such topics as tax, VAT, the DSS and employment law. The FSB will pay the costs of representation at employment tribunals over the dismissal of employees, redundancy, or accepting an employee's resignation. It also offers to pay legal costs and expenses of up to £50,000 incurred in defending a criminal case relating to business activities and up to £50,000 of legal and accountancy costs per claim in appeals to VAT tribunals and the courts. This scheme is run by the insurers Abbey Legal Protection (who are behind the Law Society's Accident Line scheme).

The motoring organisation RAC offers a personal injury scheme for motor accidents to all members and is backed by a 24-hour helpline. (It also runs a special LEI policy for cyclists at £13 for non-members and £8 for members.)

Checklist

Many of the issues that arise in relation to such services are similar to those that surround LEI. But here is a checklist:

- *Are you covered?*

  Unsurprisingly, unions tend to be limited to problems arising in the workplace. Advice is often extended to family members but it may not include partners.

- *Watch the clock*

  Generally, you have to be a union member for 13 weeks before making a claim.

- *How strong is your case?*

  Access to legal advice is often at the discretion of the union.

- *Will you get all your damages back?*

  Unions and other organisations run their cases on CFAs. Most (but not all) unions guarantee that all damages are returned to their members.

- *Can you choose your own solicitor?*

  No, but the law firms that run the scheme tend to have a long and close association with the unions (e.g. Thompsons have been advising members since 1921).

Collective conditional fee agreements

Unions and other organisations are allowed to run their own version of NWNF called 'collective CFAs'. It is worth checking whether you will receive all your damages back as the same issues apply to NWNF for union members as they do for anyone else. Most (but not all) unions will guarantee that your damages remain intact.

Collective CFAs allow unions to recover an additional amount (known as the 'notional premium') to reflect the sum that it would have cost to insure against the defendant's costs in the event of your claim failing. This represents the cost of an organisation effectively insuring its own claims against the risk of having to pay the defendant's costs in the event of a loss. The advantage of these schemes is that it allows an organisation to enter into a single CFA to cover a large number of cases.

Conditional fees have been an opportunity for unions to expand their legal services because previously they would have had to protect a member against costs which was clearly an expensive way of operating. Now they can recover the notional premium allowing them to build a legal fighting fund.

The collective CFA regulations apply to membership organisations which include not only unions but other groups, such as the RAC, who have been quick off the mark to see the advantages for its personal injury scheme.

Chapter 6
Life without lawyers

Keeping out of the courts and DIY law

There is an old legal adage that the man who represents himself has a fool for a client. Whilst true in many cases, the various established ways of resolving disputes without lawyers are increasingly building up a head of steam. It is a trend that reflects both a growing consumer confidence and a reluctance to pay lawyers for what is often seen as simple form-filling. But another motivating factor is one of plain necessity as more and more people have been denied access to the law and the legal poverty gap grows ever wider.

As said before, going through the courts should always be a last resort. More than ever greater emphasis is being placed upon what is called 'alternative dispute resolution' (ADR) which is a generic term for schemes that bypass the courts and lawyers altogether. Every year, in the region of 18,000 unhappy holidaymakers take up their grievances with their tour operators through the industry trade body's own arbitration scheme.

However, there are also in the region of 90,000 people every year who attempt to resolve disputes without the aid of a lawyer in the courts. More than half of the people who come before the Small Claims Court and tribunals are unrepresented (known as 'litigants-in-person' (or LIPs)). Indeed, the point of such courts is that they do not necessarily involve lawyers.

The wisdom of 'do-it-yourself' law depends entirely upon the nature of the complaint and the talents of the individual concerned. Even if you do decide to go to the Small Claims Court, you may well be advised to get some legal advice along the way. Most accidents that occur in the home are the result of over-ambitious DIY project attempts. Frankly, 'DIY law' can be just as treacherous without proper preparation.

This chapter will concentrate mainly on those areas of the law where it is possible to enforce legal rights without recourse to lawyers and the courts. It is concerned with ADR and, in particular, arbitration schemes – both in court (such as the Small Claims Court) and out-of-court schemes. It will also flag up non-contentious areas, such as conveyancing, Will writing and divorce, where there is a growing consumer enthusiasm to dispense with the services of professional advisers.

But first a cautionary note: lawyers – love them or hate them – are professionals and have to meet high professional standards. The vast majority are trustworthy and competent, and they have a strong code of ethics embodied in their regulations and professional indemnity insurance if all goes wrong (see chapter 1). The purpose of this chapter is to provide readers with an understanding of the considerations that need to be taken before dispensing with a lawyer's help. It does not offer advice on the legal process.

Taking on the system

LIPs can often cut a heroic figure in the popular imagination, such as the two environmental campaigners who single-handedly took on the might of the multinational fast-food company McDonald's in the longest civil action ever to grace the English Courts which ended in 1997 after two and a half years. The burger giant made one of the biggest legal mistakes of the century (even though it won the case overall) in the epic case which became known as the 'McLibel trial'. It cost the company £10 million but a lot more in terms of its reputation.

Another example which caught the imagination of the press concerned a man who lost his leg after a botched hospital operation. He sued the health authority but his case was hindered by the disappearance of his medical files until halfway through the court case and he subsequently lost his original case. After that, he was turned down by another firm of solicitors and so, without the benefit of Legal Aid, he took the case on by himself. He spent three days a week over the next nine months preparing himself for his day in the Court of Appeal and won £325,000 back in 1997.

But success stories tend to be few and far between. On a busy day the queue of LIPs at the Citizens Advice Bureau (CAB) at the Royal Courts of Justice stretches out of the door. Sadly, there is also a sizeable category of people who are doggedly convinced of the inherent rightness of their cause whatever the legal merits of their case. The habitual bringers of legal actions (known by the courts as 'vexatious litigants') have cost the government £2.3 million over the last five years in defending such actions and in 2002 those costs per year doubled over the same period. As a result, the government now has the power to issue orders requiring serial litigators to seek permission from the judge before bringing new actions.

Obsessive litigants aside, non-lawyers still fare very poorly before the courts. According to one consumer survey, the most frequently asked questions by LIPs facing their day in court are: what do I call the judge, and how do I know when I can speak? Such basic concerns reflect how little laymen know about the mysteries of the legal process.

Even in the Small Claims Courts – which are designed for non-lawyers – there are plenty of sobering stories of unrepresented people and the hurdles they face. For example, they arrive at the courtroom door armed only with their good faith and a lever arch file to discover that the other side has come armed with a couple of solicitors and a barrister.

How to complain

What do you do if your plumber has done a botched job repairing your boiler? What is your first step should your old landlord refuse to give back your deposit? Before making a complaint, you should know what your rights are and what is the correct way of enforcing them.

Instead of flying off the handle, you need to take a deep breath and work out exactly what you want – do you want your money back, compensation or simply an apology? If there are legal issues involved, you should find out just what your rights are.

A simple letter may be a good start to clearing up any dispute. For example, if you are owed money, you can write to the person who owes it. Make clear how much is owed, what it is for and the steps you have taken to recover that money. Include a warning that you will issue a County court claim if they do not pay by the date you have given. Keep a copy of the letter and any reply that you receive.

Here is an example of the sort of letter you may send, which is taken from a Court Service leaflet called *Making a claim? Some questions to ask yourself* – available at www.courtservice.gov.uk.

---

2 Spring Gardens
Anytown
A06 3BX

10 December 2003

Dear Mr Green,

You came to repair my central heating boiler on 6 October. I rang you on 7 October and again on 10 October to tell you that it was still not working properly.

You promised to call and put it right but you did not. I had to get someone else to come and repair it on 26 October which cost £157 plus VAT.

I asked you on 2 November to pay this money because it was work that you should have done. You have not paid it.

If you do not pay me the money by 19 December 2003, I will issue a County court claim against you.

Yours sincerely,

Mrs V Cross

Any letter should provide a history of the complaint, which states clearly: the nature of the service or goods that you are complaining about; the date the service was carried out or the goods purchased and the price paid. You should then outline the progress so far: the date that you first contacted him, his name and what was said. To finish, you should make clear what you would consider to be a satisfactory outcome and when by. Keep a copy of the letter.

Tips on complaining

Make sure that you are aware of what your rights are. If there are legal issues involved, find out whether the law is on your side.

- Know what you want to achieve. Think about what you are looking to recover. Do you want damages or will an apology do?
- Don't hang about. If you have a valid complaint, then you should act promptly.
- Deal with the right person. A quick phone call should identify the correct person who is responsible for complaints in any company. You should keep a record of anyone that you speak to and what was said.
- Put your complaint in writing. Keep copies of any letters you send.
- Put your case together. Make sure that you keep hold of any evidence, for example, photographs of damage caused, a record of expenses incurred and invoices.
- Do not be put off.

Will you get your money back?

Generally, your solicitor will advise you on your prospects of success. If you are not represented, you should bear in mind who you are dealing with – be it person, firm or company.

Check if this person, firm or company:

- is unemployed;
- is bankrupt;
- has no money of his/its own;
- has no personal property and nothing else of value (such as a car) which is not hired, subject to a hire purchase or lease agreement;
- has ceased to trade; or
- has other debts to pay.

If the person is bankrupt, you will probably not get your money back. You can contact the Insolvency Service (see Appendix for its contact details). It will be able to establish whether the person is bankrupt or the company is in 'compulsory liquidation' (i.e. it has stopped trading and probably has neither money nor assets).

If the person you are claiming from has already been taken to court by others and has not paid, then you may also have little chance of getting your money. You can find out if he has any outstanding court orders (called 'judgments') against him by writing to Registry Trust Limited (see Appendix for their contact details). You will have to make a payment (£4.50 at present) for each name you are interested in.

Should you win your case, the court still does not guarantee that you will get you money back if, for example, you were chasing money owed to you.

Do you have a small claim?

It is a procedure where DIY legal representation is commonplace. Whether you are owed money, are pursuing your landlord who has refused to return your deposit, or if you have been ripped off by a cowboy builder, then the Small Claims Court may be the answer to your problems. The usual court formalities are dispensed with, for example, there is no bench, no witness box and parties normally sit round a table. Small claims proceedings take place in the County court; to find your nearest, check your local telephone directory.

A judge recently described the Small Claims Court as being the 'Ford Mondeo' of the civil justice system, as opposed to the 'expensive Rolls-Royce service' of the High Court, and the fast track trials with a value of £5,000 to £15,000 being 'middle of the range Volvo justice'. (See chapter 2 for further information on the different types of hearing.) The average length of a small claims hearing is just 61 minutes. The normal time from start to finish (or from the issue of proceedings to the court hearing) is about six months.

What is its jurisdiction?

It is appropriate for a small claim where you are claiming money or property worth £5,000 or less. If your case involves personal injury or housing disrepair it will only be heard in the Small Claims Court if you are claiming £1,000 or less. A judge has the power to refer your case to the Small Claims Court if he thinks it is necessary, even if your claim is for more than £5,000, for example, if the parties do not have solicitors.

Law without the lawyers?

Although most small claims cases are heard without lawyers, it may be necessary to check with a lawyer to ensure that you have a good case. Despite the work of the court being deemed arbitration, normal legal principles apply and it is important that you make your case in law. Although you may not be instructing a lawyer to conduct your claim, it may be worth taking advantage of the free legal advice offered by any decent solicitor in an initial interview to assess whether you have a claim. If you have to pay, agree a fixed fee.

Can you represent yourself?

Most small claims cases are heard without lawyers. According to the Legal Services Commission (LSC), 'As a general rule, if your claim is for a sum over £5,000 and particularly if it includes a claim for compensation, it is advisable to seek the advice of a solicitor.' In a simple case for debt, for example, you may not consider it necessary to consult a solicitor. If the amount you are claiming is £5,000 or less and is defended, you may want to take someone for moral support or even someone to speak on your behalf if you are feeling intimidated, such as a friend or advice worker. The norm is for small companies to be represented by directors or sales managers. There are no legal costs orders made, so if your opponent arrives with his legal team he will have to pay, win or lose.

Can you afford to go to court?

You may have to pay a fee to start your claim. Fees are proportionate to the amount claimed. (At the time of publication, for a claim for money of up to £3,000 the court fee is £30 and for a claim of up to £5,000 it may be £120.) There are exemptions if, for example, you are receiving Income Support. If the claim is defended you may have to pay further fees which you will recover if you win. You may be allowed to recover some costs for time lost at work but it may not necessarily cover the total amount lost.

Other expenses

If the claim is defended, you may need, for example, witnesses or experts' reports and will have to pay their costs which may be recovered if you win. If your claim is for a specified amount, and the defendant is an individual who defends the claim, the claim may be transferred to his local court. So there could also be travel costs. If you have a solicitor and instruct him, you will usually have to pay even if you win the case.

If the judge decides in your favour ordering the defendant to pay you, the court will not automatically take steps to ensure that the money is paid. If the defendant does not pay, you will need to take action for which you will have to pay another fee.

For more information see www.courtservice.gov.uk where the leaflet *The Small Claims Track* is available online as well as Lawpack's *Small Claims Guide*.

Note: if you are chasing a debt, the government has launched a new service, Money Claim Online that allows consumers and small businesses to sue debtors for claims below £100,000 and to engage the services of a County court bailiff.

Users can register at www.courtservice.gov.uk/mcol and they can, by creating a user ID and password, securely pay court fees online with a credit card. (At the time of publication, the minimum fee is £27 and increases in proportion to the size of the claim.) Ministers reckon that 25,000 claims will be made in its first year of operation. A judge can examine the claim and make a judgment online if a defendant admits to the debt or fails to respond to the claim. Defendants have 14 days to respond to his decision, after which a warrant is issued and the bailiffs can go in to recover the money.

Alternative dispute resolution

As said before, going through the courts should always be a last resort. There is a far greater emphasis than ever before placed on solutions that fall outside the legal system. It can be far cheaper for both consumers and the businesses themselves and is a considerably less stressful experience. The generic name for such an approach is 'alternative dispute resolution' (ADR) and such schemes use an arbitrator or ombudsman (an official appointed by the government to investigate complaints) to help you reach an agreement.

If you wish to use a scheme you should contact the business against which you have the complaint and find out if it is a member of a trade body. If so, your next step is to contact the trade association and find out if it has a code of conduct and a conciliation or arbitration scheme. There are no guarantees that members will stick to the code but the ultimate sanction is that they will be expelled from their trade association.

It is a cheap (and often free) way of resolving your dispute. There is no need for lawyers to be involved and it is usually a simple 'papers-only' process without any hearing. On the other hand, it can have its drawbacks depending on your circumstances: you may feel that your complaint is so severe that you want it to be heard in court. Also there may be cost considerations: there is no limit on compensation for a negligence action before the courts whereas an arbitration scheme will have limits. Another consideration is that your case may hang on the evidence of a witness and only a court can order such a witness to attend. One critical consideration is that an arbitrator's decision is legally binding which means that the option of going to court will be closed.

■ Conciliation

The first step in the arbitration process whereby a trade association will appoint a middleman, usually a member of the association, to investigate your claim. You and the business in question will be asked to give written details of the complaint and the conciliator will give an opinion. It is not a binding decision and you can still opt for the courts. If you disagree with the opinion offered, you can then proceed to the arbitration stage or consider suing in court. There is usually no charge for conciliation.

■ Arbitration

Here both you and the company usually agree to accept the decision of the arbitrator as legally binding, which means that you cannot go to the courts (unless it is to enforce the award if the other party does not pay up). More often than not, the arbitrator will be a member of the Chartered Institute of Arbitrators and as such will be independent of the company. It is a paper-based process which means that a decision is arrived at by reviewing any written evidence provided by you and the other side. There is no hearing to attend. The decision is confidential and cannot be made public without the other side's agreement.

A contract for services or a delivery note may well include an 'arbitration clause' stating that you will refer any dispute to arbitration, so check the paperwork. Although this is binding once you have signed the agreement, if the total cost is below the small claims limit (£5,000) you cannot be forced to arbitrate unless you gave your agreement after the dispute arose.

Arbitration can be an effective and economical alternative to the courts. It is an informal mechanism for reaching a decision on a dispute that binds both parties. (The procedure before the Small Claims Court is also described as 'arbitration', although it is part of the County court. However, it is a more relaxed consumer-friendly version of the courts – see page 125).

The Chartered Institute of Arbitrators administers over 100 different consumer dispute resolution schemes. Basically, arbitration is a set procedure that takes place under the body's rules which the parties sign up to. The whole point of such a scheme is that it is more cost effective and quicker than litigation.

These schemes are more widespread than you may think. For example, the Association of British Travel Agents (ABTA) has over 2,000 members with more than 7,000 high street shops. Some 18,000 complaints are made to the scheme each year and about

1,500 are arbitrated. The next biggest area for arbitration is housing-related claims. The Royal Institution of Chartered Surveyors (RICS) has 70,000 members on its scheme, which deals with problems over surveys, and there are 44,000 mortgage lenders and advisers registered to the Mortgage Code. Typically, there are between 100 and 150 housing-related arbitrations every year.

Generally, arbitration is a paper-based process designed to keep costs down, but there are some exceptions in more complex cases, such as complaints against surveyors. It is a simple, straightforward procedure and, reassuringly, some 80 per cent of all arbitrations are decided in favour of the consumer.

The parties to a dispute are aware of the maximum cost of the procedure at the outset, and the tailor-made rules leave no room for surprises. You may have to pay a fee but you should be able to recover it if you are successful. In the majority of schemes you as the consumer do not pay any fees. (To give you an example of how fees may vary, at the time of publication the fee for the ABTA scheme is £78, whereas the RICS scheme can cost £750.) The arbitrator has the power to award costs under statute.

There will also be tight deadlines. Typically, a defendant company has 28 days to consider any evidence put forward by you. You will then have 14 working days to respond to the defence statement. According to the Chartered Institute of Arbitrators, the usual time frame is three months from application to completion.

A list of ADR groups can be found in the Appendix at the back of the book, which features organisations that run schemes for all kinds of disputes from dry-cleaning disasters to lost luggage. This non-exhaustive list comes from the European Extra-Judicial Network (EEJ-Net) and their website (www.eej-net.org.uk) contains more information about the individual schemes. Most of these organisations are part of the EEJ scheme which allows Europe-wide dispute resolution.

The DTI's Consumer Gateway provides links to bodies not part of EEJ-Net (see www.consumer.gov.uk). For more information about arbitration, The Chartered Institute of Arbitrators website (www.arbitrators.org) is a good place to start. It administers the vast majority of schemes and has details online. The National Association of Citizens Advice Bureaux's Advice Guide is another useful site (www.adviceguide.org.uk).

■ Mediation

A mediator will help you and the other party negotiate an agreement and will act as a go-between if you don't want to meet. If the other party agrees to mediation, you will both be asked to give details of the dispute, including copies of any evidence. You will also be asked to sign a mediation agreement giving a framework for the negotiation. The mediator may arrange joint or separate meetings and will help you to identify the strengths and weaknesses in your case. If an agreement is reached, you will both be asked to meet to draft the terms of the settlement. This will be legally binding unless you state otherwise and will prevent you from taking court action, except to enforce the award.

Mediation can be expensive but you may be able to apply to the Community Legal Service (CLS) for help under the Legal Help scheme or the publicly funded Legal Representation scheme (see chapter 3).

To find out more about mediation, visit www.mediationuk.org.uk. The organisation is a national voluntary organisation 'dedicated to developing constructive means of resolving conflicts in communities'.

Ombudsman schemes

A number of services will have an ombudsman scheme that you can use. An ombudsman is an official appointed to investigate complaints by the public against government departments or professional organisations. For example, services provided by insurance companies, and banks and building societies are now all covered by the Financial Ombudsman Service. Other examples are the Legal Services Ombudsman (LSO) (see chapter 7) and the Ombudsman for Estate Agents.

You will only be able to refer the matter to the ombudsman after you have completed any internal complaints procedures that are available. All schemes require that complaints must be sent in within a reasonable time. Usually there is a fixed time limit and you will need to give written details of your complaint, together with copies of any of your evidence. In some schemes the ombudsman will first try to achieve an agreed solution by acting as a mediator between the complainant and the organisation concerned. The ombudsman will make a recommendation or a ruling, which is usually accepted by the supplier, but is not legally binding. Hence, you can still take court action if you are not satisfied with the decision. However, the court will take the ombudsman's ruling into account when deciding your claim. All the ombudsman schemes are free. A full list of ombudsman schemes are available at www.bioa.org.uk (the British and Irish Ombudsman Association).

An alternative dispute resolution checklist

- *Is alternative dispute resolution available?*

  Check if the company or trader against whom you are complaining is a member of a trade association and also whether the trade association has a dispute resolution scheme. You can ring or check on the websites listed in the Appendix.

- *Are you happy for an arbitrator to have the final say?*

  Remember that many ADR decisions will be legally binding and will prevent you from taking court action (with the exception of enforcing an award if a defendant company is not forthcoming).

- *What is the likely value of your claim?*

  If your claim is over £5,000, you should discuss the possibility of ADR with your solicitor or legal adviser. If it is less, then you should weigh up the pros and cons of ADR versus the Small Claims Courts.

- *Are the courts more appropriate than alternative dispute resolution?*

  If you have a reluctant witness, only a court can compel him to attend. There is no limit on the amount of compensation you can claim for in, for example, negligence action in court.

Going it alone

These are some areas of the law that have traditionally been the preserve of lawyers, and are now increasingly being taken on by people without any (or much) help from lawyers. As to why, it is partly down to increased consumer confidence, concerns about legal costs and out of sheer necessity.

Away from the courts, there is a trend for non-lawyers to tackle areas of the law such as Will writing, conveyancing and even divorce. The Internet is revolutionising many of the more form-based legal processes – most notably divorce and Wills – and lawyers online will offer a halfway house between going it alone and putting yourself completely in the hands of your lawyers. For example, one solicitor-run website offers an 'e-divorce' with a free Will thrown in for £85. You are given the paperwork, online advice and the rest is up to you.

There are also numerous guides or packs offering legal documentation on sale at high street stationers promising easy-to-follow instruction through legal issues. There are huge pitfalls to be aware of so it is vital to read the instructions carefully. If a Will is not witnessed properly, it means that the intestacy rules apply and your estate passes automatically to your next of kin and not, for example, to your long-term girlfriend or boyfriend.

Wills

Drawing up a Will can be a relatively straightforward exercise and in most situations it should take no more than an hour or two to do. The cost savings of doing it yourself rather than hiring a solicitor, whose usual costs can be anything between £70 for a simple Will to £1,000 for a more complex case, must be set against the risk of making mistakes.

Why make a Will?

Three in four people under 45 years old (and one in two over-45s) fail to make a Will. Understandably, people don't like to contemplate their own mortality. But the consequences of dying intestate (not having a Will) can be dire for those you leave behind. Fixed legal rules determine who benefits on intestacy and they are not always the people you may want. For example, if you are married you may think that your spouse inherits everything. Wrong. If there are children or other relatives, your widow or widower inherits the first £125,000 outright, but only half of any remaining assets. The rest will be shared equally between your children. If you are not married but you have a partner, under the rules of intestacy your partner will not be able to obtain anything. Another compelling reason for a Will is that it is an opportunity to organise your estate and limit any inheritance tax liability.

When should you consider a DIY Will?

Drawing up your own Will should only be considered in reasonably straightforward cases. The charity Will Aid (backed by the likes of ActionAid, British Red Cross and Save the Children) advises people to take proper advice from a solicitor.

It is best to take legal advice when you have a complex estate, for example, where you run your own company, or have foreign property or assets abroad. Alternatively, if you have children from a previous marriage, it is best to take advice. If the value of your estate is over £255,000 – the inheritance tax threshold – then there will be tax considerations that you should explore with a professional.

How much will it cost?

DIY guides and kits are available from the bigger high street stationers and post offices, for example, Lawpack's *Last Will & Testament Kit* and the *Wills, Power of Attorney & Probate* guide. You can expect to pay a solicitor less than £100 for a single Will and £120 for a joint Will if the estates are simple.

There are also a number of companies that specialise in Will writing as well as being independent financial consultants. High street banks offer Will-making services and can offer competitive rates for customers who take out, for example, life assurance policies. Banks may act as executor and you should find out how much this service will cost. Under the government's much-heralded 'Tesco law' proposals (which would allow banks, building societies and supermarkets to offer legal services) the prospect of being able to have a Will drawn up at these outlets has been heavily flagged up.

Most high street law firms will draft Wills and Will Aid has its own online solicitor locator – www.willaid.org.uk – which will identify your nearest solicitor.

Note: Some lawyers claim to make almost as much money from resolving the problems created by DIY Wills than they do from drawing them up! Care must be taken to heed the instructions as not doing so may prove an expensive mistake.

Probate

In the shock of bereavement, many families instruct a solicitor to wind up someone's estate (the money, property and possessions left) by collecting in all the money, paying any debts and distributing the estate to those people entitled to it. More often than not family members refer the matter to the solicitor who wrote the Will. The term 'probate' refers to the issuing of a legal document ('a grant of representation') by the Probate Registry to one or more people authorising them to do this.

One can expect to pay anything from £60 to £120 an hour for a probate clerk or an experienced solicitor at a law firm. On average, legal costs can be somewhere between two per cent or 3.5 per cent of the total of an estate – and so beneficiaries of a £200,000 estate may lose £6,000 in fees.

Again, it can seem a lot of money for a relatively straightforward process. There are guides available for DIY probate which can provide guidance on the process and the forms to obtain. Probate registries also provide a pack for those who do not want to take professional advice. They include a leaflet which is available online at www.probate1.com. The average estate takes about six months to administer and DIY executors need plenty of time and patience as there can be scores of letters to write, telephone calls to make and forms to complete.

Professional help will be needed in some situations: where larger estates worth more than £255,000 create potential inheritance tax liabilities and professional help may assist in reducing these significantly; where the beneficiaries have fallen out or where a Will is disputed. Even so, you may be able to limit a solicitor's involvement to one or two hours.

Divorce

DIY divorce is not for everyone. For example, many people qualify for Legal Aid – see chapter 3.

In general, DIY divorce is best suited to cases where the spouses are agreed that they want a divorce and where there will be a reasonable degree of co-operation. It is an unwise choice if the other spouse has decided not to co-operate or even to defend the divorce. This type of situation normally requires legal help.

How do you proceed?

If the case is suitable for a DIY divorce the necessary papers can be obtained from any local County court that does divorce. Lawpack's *Separation & Divorce Kit* also provides the necessary forms as well as explaining the legal, financial and practical issues involved.

There are three main issues in divorce. First, there is the divorce itself, which starts with issuing a divorce petition and ends with a decree absolute terminating the marriage, enabling either party to remarry if they so wish. Second, if the spouses wish to resolve financial matters between them then this is done in what are called 'ancillary relief proceedings'. (There is no reason why this cannot be done by agreement but in the last resort a judge can be asked to decide if no agreement is reached.) Third, there may be a dispute about children such as where they are going to live. Most divorcing couples settle issues relating to children without any intervention by a court.

What are the dangers?

By the term 'DIY divorce', most people consider the first of the above three issues. However, it is wise to deal with the financial settlement and most people do not realise that when a couple divorce they have potential financial claims against the other, for example, for capital, such as a share in a house or savings, for maintenance or there can be claims against a pension. These claims do not come to an end when the decree absolute has been pronounced in a divorce. Most people who conduct their own divorce are not aware of this.

For example, take a husband and wife who obtained a DIY divorce in 1995 and H remarried in 1996. At the moment H remarried his financial claims against his wife lapsed. However, W did not remarry and her claims remain open and she may make these claims years after the marriage was ended by decree absolute. If a court is asked to decide such claims then it will make its decision based on financial circumstances as they are at the time of making the decision and not as they were at the time of the divorce or the separation. Therefore assets acquired after the divorce are taken into account.

How much will it cost?

In the case of a DIY divorce the costs of a divorce amount to little more than the court fees, presently about £180 to issue a divorce petition and £30 to apply for a decree absolute. (If a person instructs a solicitor to obtain the divorce, there are additional legal fees, normally in the region of about £400 plus VAT.) Issues relating to children do not need to be dealt with in most cases because divorcing couples usually resolve them by agreement.

However, dealing with financial issues relating to the divorce is vital, even in one where there are no assets. It is not suitable for DIY but there is no reason why this cannot be done by agreement and then it is just a question of getting a solicitor to draw up the agreement and to submit it to the court. Costs would be modest: a court fee of £30 to file and £200-300 for solicitors' fees. If there is no agreement, then a solicitor will charge on a time basis and it will cost as long as it takes to reach agreement.

[source: *David Terry of Terry & Co solicitors*]

Conveyancing

Conveyancing is the legal process relating to the buying and selling of a house. It may be glorified form-filling but a house purchase is the biggest financial investment that many of us will make and it is crucial that we get it right.

What is the legal process?

Basically, the conveyancing (i.e. transferring ownership) involves checking the title of the property, making Land Registry and local authority searches, creating a legal contract and handling 'discharge' paperwork depending on any change of mortgage lender or variation in a loan. According to one estimate, the workload for one person would be somewhere between 12 and 15 hours spread out over the six to eight weeks that a house move takes.

What are the limits?

If you are taking out a mortgage, your lender may insist on using a lawyer. However, DIY conveyancers can still do most of the work themselves and only pay for a solicitor to handle the transaction. If your property is held on leasehold and a new lease needs to be drawn up or an old one amended, then you would be advised to see a solicitor.

Chapter 7
What to do if it all goes wrong

Even in the best solicitors' firms, mistakes can happen. If you are troubled by some part of your solicitor's conduct, always try to sort it out directly with him first. Explain why you are unhappy and what you would like to be done about it. In most situations, it will be possible to nip the problem in the bud. If you are concerned, never delay because the issue may be easily resolved and, if you need to pursue a complaint, there can be strict deadlines.

All firms should have their own internal complaints procedure. Refer to your client care letter which should identify the partner at the firm responsible for dealing with complaints. If it doesn't, phone up and ask. Again, explain what the problem is and how you would like it to be sorted out.

If, having done this, you are still not happy, then contact the solicitors' watchdog, the Office for the Supervision of Solicitors (OSS). Strict time limits apply. The office can deal with complaints of incompetence and shoddy work but it cannot handle complaints of negligence ('negligence' has a special meaning here – see page 147). If you still have problems, then you can take the matter to the Legal Services Ombudsman (LSO).

There has been much justified criticism about the inability of the legal profession to deal effectively with the rising tide of complaints regarding lawyers. This is a debate that is frequently aired in the running battle between the Law Society and the Department for Constitutional Affairs (formerly the Lord Chancellor's Department) over the Law Society's twin roles of trade union and regulator – and whether it should be stripped of the latter.

There are approximately 14,000 complaints made against solicitors each year. The former LSO, Ann Abraham, was an outspoken critic of the way in which the legal profession dealt with complaints. She described the OSS's performance as 'consistently shaky' and claimed that only 58 per cent of complaints were handled satisfactorily in 2001. Efforts have been made to deal with the problem that, at its worst, led to a backlog of 13,000 pending complaints (see note below). So far the Law Society has succeeded in staving off threats to strip it of its powers – but for how long?

The bottom line is that the OSS has great powers at its disposal to deal with complaints – certainly when compared to most other watchdogs. In particular, it has the power to order compensation of up to £5,000 (£15,000 from 2004), reduce legal bills (to zero if necessary), and report the firm to the Solicitors Disciplinary Tribunal (see page 149). But do not expect too much. The OSS says that its emphasis nowadays is very much on achieving reconciliation between lawyer and client. And despite compensation being substantially upped in recent years – from a meagre £1,000 to £15,000 – the average award remains in the region of £300. Awards of over £1,000 tend to be limited to those cases where the performance of the solicitor is, in the words of the OSS, 'abysmal', leaving the client in 'anguish'.

Note: the OSS now aims to deal with 50 per cent of their investigations into poor service and professional misconduct within three months, and 80 per cent within six months.

Problems with solicitors

How to complain about your solicitor

Discuss the problem

If it is a problem relating to the service you have received, discuss the problem with either the solicitor directly or, if that is awkward, the partner in his firm responsible for complaints. All firms must have their own complaints procedures. The client care letter should identify them. If he is a sole practitioner (SP), then he may have an arrangement with another local firm or with the local Law Society to deal with complaints.

Explain the nature of your complaint and what you want to be done about it. Take notes of your conversation and ask the solicitor to supply you with a copy of his complaints procedure if it is not offered to you. This should confirm the name of the person at the firm who will be dealing with your complaint, the action he will be taking and the date by which he will do this.

Put your complaint in writing

Any complaint should eventually be recorded in writing. Your solicitor will then have a record of the details. You should keep a copy of your letter. If you don't want to write a letter to your solicitor, then the OSS has its own resolution form which is available on its website (www.oss.lawsociety.org.uk) as well as at your local Citizens Advice Bureau (CAB). Do not use it if you are complaining about someone else's lawyer.

Referring the case to the OSS

You should contact the OSS when:

1. you haven't received a detailed reply to your initial complaint from your solicitor within a reasonable time, say 28 days;
2. you haven't been able to sort out your complaint with your solicitor; and
3. your complaint is about a solicitor's conduct.

It is important that you contact the OSS within six months of the matter you are complaining about. If you leave it any longer, it may decide not to investigate your complaint.

If you feel you have grounds for complaint about your solicitor, then the nature of your problem will determine your course of action and the kind of remedy you can expect.

What are you complaining about?

The bill

There are procedures in place for lawyers' fees to be challenged without too much difficulty provided that the challenge is mounted promptly, i.e. no later then one month after the bill is delivered. It becomes increasingly difficult as time passes.

A solicitor's bill is supposedly required to contain sufficient detail to enable you to assess whether the charge is reasonable or not. A client is entitled to ask for a detailed bill but, be warned, it may well be higher than the one originally delivered and will replace the original bill. There may be a perfectly good reason why your bill is higher than anticipated as cases can take unpredictable and expensive turns.

If there is a line in the bill stipulating that an extra 60 per cent has been charged for 'care and conduct' of the case, this is the uplift (see chapter 2). You will only have to pay this if you were notified at the onset of the case.

If you consider your solicitor's charges to be too high, first you should complain directly to your solicitor as soon as possible. Most complaints are settled this way by agreement.

If you need to challenge the bill, you must inform your solicitor within a month of receiving it that you want the Law Society to assess it. Ask him to apply to the OSS for a 'remuneration certificate' or for a contentious work, the courts can check if your bill is fair through the 'assessment' procedure.

Remuneration certificate

If there are no court proceedings involved, you can ask for the solicitor to obtain a certificate of remuneration from the Law Society in order for it to check your bill. This is a free service provided by the OSS. You must act quickly, though. The request must be made within one month of delivery of the bill – this also applies to solicitors' bills that arrive during the life of a case.

Unless your solicitor's costs have been taken from money recovered, the bill should not be paid in full – but 50 per cent of the costs, all of the VAT and all of the expenses will have to be paid before the solicitor is required to apply for a certificate. If your solicitor takes his costs from money being held for you (e.g. if you are selling a house) and does not tell you of your right to ask for a certificate, you must query the bill in writing within three months of receiving the bill. If your solicitor takes his costs from money being held for you and tells you of your right to ask for a certificate, you must ask for it within one month of the date you received the bill.

The Law Society will decide if the bill is reasonable or, if not, what is a reasonable amount for the client to have to pay. The decision is not binding on either party but is usually accepted by solicitors.

If you fail to pay the solicitor's bill, it is likely the solicitor will sue for recovery. You can then file a defence challenging the amount claimed as being unreasonable and a procedure similar to remuneration certificate assessment will follow.

Assessment (formerly known as 'taxation')

If the work did involve court proceedings, you can ask the court to decide on the reasonableness or otherwise of the solicitor's bill. In a process known as 'detailed assessment', the solicitor will be required to produce a detailed bill which you can challenge item by item. The procedure involves you issuing an application in the court in which the proceedings ran.

You should be careful because having the courts check your legal bills can be an expensive business. Even if your bill is reduced, you may have to pay your own costs and your solicitor's costs. If the solicitor's bill is reduced in total by more than one fifth, the solicitor will have to pay the costs of the application, otherwise you must pay those costs. A simple bill can be dealt with in a couple of hours whereas a complex bill can take days and can end up overshadowing the amount in dispute. It is a galling thought that you can succeed in reducing your lawyer's bill by £3,000 (from £20,000 to £17,000) and be stuck with a new solicitor's bill plus the old one from your overcharging solicitor.

Again, there are strict time limits. If you apply to the court within one month of having received your bill, the court will always allow assessment to go ahead. If you apply between up to one year of receiving the bill and you have not paid it yet, the court may order assessment but it doesn't have to. If you have paid your bill and it is more than 12 months since you received it, you can no longer challenge the bill.

The procedure can be used even if court proceedings were not involved but it can be somewhat cumbersome and the client should seek expert or professional advice. Your local County court or the Supreme Court Costs Office can advise about the procedural requirements for the application.

Note: Advice on solicitors' bills may be obtained from Fellows of the Association of Law Costs Draftsmen (ALCD) who are regarded as experts in the field of solicitors' costs by the courts. It should be remembered that most law costs draftsmen are employed, either directly or casually, by solicitors and you should make sure that the costs draftsman does not undertake work for the solicitor concerned. Details of members of the ALCD may be obtained from www.alcd.org.uk. Please note than only Fellows of the ALCD are regarded as experts.

Poor service

If your solicitor never returns your calls, contact him directly. It may be that he doesn't want you to incur the cost of him answering your calls when there is no news. In most cases, a frank exchange of views will clear the air. If there is a problem, then try the firm's complaints procedures.

If this does not resolve the problem, the OSS deals with situations where your solicitor fails to do what you have instructed him to, or where there are unreasonable delays, or perhaps he has given you inaccurate or incomplete information.

The OSS can reduce your solicitor's bill; order him to pay you compensation of up to £5,000 (expected to be £15,000 from 2004); or tell him to correct a mistake and pay any costs involved. However, the OSS claims that the most likely result is that the client and solicitor will reach an agreement. The OSS now focuses mainly on conciliation between parties and, if an award is made, the average sum is only about £300. If you are still unhappy, you can take your case to the LSO (you must have pursued your complaint with the OSS first). Approximately seven per cent of cases dealt with by the OSS are subsequently referred to the LSO. The LSO can then make a recommendation – there is no limit on the amount awarded and it is only a recommendation.

Negligence

Should your slip and trip claim fall three years after the accident due to the mistake of your solicitor, it will become 'statute-barred' (i.e. it cannot proceed because the time laid down in the statute of limitations has expired). Negligence has a special meaning in law – there has to be a breakdown (or 'breach') of a duty of care owed to you. You may be able to sue your solicitor if that negligence has meant that you have lost money or had to spend money trying to put things right. Solicitors are covered by professional indemnity insurance (see chapter 1) to cover valid claims.

A compensation claim will seek to put you in the position you would have been in had your solicitor not acted negligently. So if the court disallowed your slip and trip claim because your solicitor carelessly missed the three-year deadline, the court will assess what award you would have received. Your solicitor would then have to pay that sum plus any legal costs.

There is common ground between negligence and poor service, and sometimes the OSS can deal with the complaint. However, it cannot decide that a solicitor has been negligent – this is a matter for the courts or the solicitor's insurers.

You will need to ask the firm who their insurers are. The OSS may refer you to a solicitor on its negligence panel scheme. The first hour is free and it will try to establish whether your solicitor was negligent. If it considers that to be the case, it will inform you of what you should do next. The OSS will not make such a referral if you have already asked for independent legal advice. If you think your solicitor has been negligent, you should get independent legal advice, as there are time limits for making complaints.

The first thing to do is to contact your solicitor and tell him that you plan to make a claim. He will then tell his insurers who will carry out an investigation and decide if it is appropriate to settle a claim. If they do, they will decide what amount is appropriate. If not, you may have to go to court and you may have to pay court costs.

Professional misconduct, theft and dishonesty

If there has been professional misconduct and your solicitor is in breach of the Law Society's rules, the OSS can investigate your claim. But even if it establishes misconduct, it can't award compensation. However, it can discipline the solicitor involved. There is a range of sanctions – one involves placing a 'condition' on a solicitor's practising certificate preventing him from dealing with certain types of work.

The most serious or persistent cases of solicitors' misconduct – such as suspected dishonesty, a criminal conviction or mishandling clients' money – are reported by the OSS to the Solicitors Disciplinary Tribunal. The tribunal has the power to fine the solicitor, suspend him or take away his practising certificate. The tribunal is independent and holds public hearings which are often reported in the local press.

In the year ending April 2003, the tribunal made orders against 220 solicitors – in about one third of the cases, the solicitor was ordered to be struck off and another 39 were suspended indefinitely. 89 solicitors were also fined, with fines ranging from £250 to £17,500.

Offences considered to be professional misconduct are as follows:

- Your solicitor not treating your personal affairs as confidential.
- A failure to pay money over to you or to prepare accounts in order to show what is owed to you.
- There is a conflict of interest (i.e. he has acted for you and your opponent on related matters).
- Your money has been stolen or used without your permission.

In cases of theft and dishonesty, if you have suffered a loss or hardship as a result of your solicitor's dishonesty, you can apply for a grant from the Compensation Fund. This is run by the OSS on behalf of the Law Society. The OSS has the power to shut down a firm. An award from the Compensation Fund can replace the money that a solicitor has stolen or pay legal costs which you have had to pay when you applied for a grant.

What if you are complaining about someone else's solicitor?

The OSS can only help if the situation involves professional misconduct as opposed to poor service given by someone else's solicitor. Before you write to the OSS, they recommend that you discuss your concerns with either your own solicitor or the OSS helpline (see Appendix for details).

If your complaint is about the way a solicitor has dealt with the estate of someone who has died, the OSS can investigate this if the solicitor is an executor (i.e. named in the Will to deal with the dead person's affairs) and you have been left a share of the estate, as opposed to a fixed sum or a particular gift.

Changing your solicitor

If you believe that the service of your lawyer is poor or just plain awful, then your first wish will be to change solicitors. You can always take your work to another firm but first you should always raise the issues directly with your solicitor.

Certainly, changing solicitors is not a decision to be taken lightly. Most solicitors are perfectly competent but also there will be a certain amount of duplication of work so you may end up paying twice.

It may be worth taking a second opinion if there are no substantive grounds for your loss of faith, perhaps from your local CAB or sound out another lawyer.

Be aware that if you owe your solicitor any fees for work that he has already completed, he is perfectly within his rights to hang on to any of your property in his possession. This will include any money, documents or deeds. This is known as the 'solicitors' lien'. This may be problematic if you want to challenge the bill by a remuneration certificate – you will have to pay the bill in full but clearly state that the payment was made without prejudice to your right to ask for a remuneration certificate.

There are ways in which you can have your property returned without paying, for example, the Law Society can recommend its release subject to an agreement to pay the fee. Your new solicitor will advise you.

Still not satisfied?

If you are not happy with the way that the OSS has dealt with your complaint or with the decision that they have taken, you can refer the matter to the LSO (at the time of going to press it is Zahida Manzoor) who oversees the way the OSS and the Law Society handles complaints about solicitors.

Once the OSS has told you of its final decision in writing, you normally have three months to refer the case to the LSO. If you miss this deadline, the LSO will not normally consider your case unless there are special reasons for doing so – these are circumstances beyond your control that prevented you from referring your case to the LSO in time, for example, you or a member of your close family may have been seriously ill.

The LSO cannot look into the following types of complaints: compensation fund applications, remuneration certificate applications, the closing down of a solicitor's practice by the OSS and deposit interest certificates (relating to your entitlement if a solicitor holds money for you).

If the LSO finds that your complaint has not been properly handled, she can recommend that the OSS reconsider your complaint. She also has the power to recommend or order that either the OSS or the solicitor pay compensation. There is no limit to the amount of compensation that the LSO can recommend or order.

Problems with barristers and other professionals

Barristers

Solicitors tend to bear the brunt of the public's discontent for two obvious reasons – they outnumber their peers at the Bar ten to one and they are generally the public face of the profession. But if you have a complaint against a barrister who, for example, you have taken specialist advice from, the Bar Council runs its own complaints scheme through their Complaints Commissioner.

First of all talk to your solicitor, if you have one, and establish whether he agrees with your assessment of the situation and, if so, whether he can resolve it properly.

Again, there are strict time limits. Normally, you must complain to the Bar Council within six months of the complaint arising. The Bar has the discretion to look at later complaints if they are particularly serious or if there is a good reason for the delay.

Basically, the scheme covers professional misconduct and inadequate professional service. Professional misconduct is defined as 'a serious error or misbehaviour by a barrister which may well involve some element of dishonesty or serious incompetence'. This may include misleading the court, failure to keep affairs confidential, leaving a case without good reason at short notice and acting against a client's instructions or best interests. The Bar Council has a number of penalties from simply giving advice, fining, ordering a barrister to repay, to disbarring the barrister (i.e. so that he ceases to be a barrister).

The scheme also covers less serious complaints, such as inadequate professional service. This covers delays in dealing with papers, poor or inadequate work on a case and serious rudeness to the client. In these situations the Bar Council can require a barrister to apologise to a client, to repay fees or to pay compensation of up to £5,000. The Bar can deal with a barrister for both misconduct and inadequate professional service in respect of the same complaint.

If the Commissioner considers that the complaint may be justified, he will refer it to the Professional Conduct and Complaints Committee (PCC) for consideration. If you are dissatisfied with the Bar Council's handling of a complaint, you will be able to refer the matter to the LSO.

What if your claim failed because your barrister was hopeless and failed to perform adequately in the courtroom? Until recently there was little you could do as barristers enjoyed a centuries-old immunity from negligence claims. The situation used to be that barristers could be sued for negligence in advice or paperwork, but not over anything done in court or 'intimately connected' with court proceedings. However, the House of Lords has since ended the rule that barristers and solicitors are immune from lawsuits for their negligent work done in court.

Other professionals

As to how complaints are dealt with by other legal personnel such as licensed conveyancers and legal executives, contact the Council for Licensed Conveyancers and the Institute of Legal Executives (see Appendix for details).

Appendix

Solicitors' practice rules: Practice Rule 15 (costs information and client care)

When informing the client about costs:

(a) Costs information must not be inaccurate or misleading.

(b) Any costs information required to be given by the code [of the conduct of solicitors] must be given clearly, in a way and at a level which is appropriate to the particular client. Any terms with which the client may be unfamiliar, for example, 'disbursement', should be explained.

(c) The information…should be given to a client at the outset of, and at appropriate stages throughout, the matter. All information given orally should be confirmed in writing to the client as soon as possible.

Advance costs information – general

The overall costs

(a) The solicitor should give the client the best information possible about the likely overall costs, including a breakdown between fees, VAT and disbursements.

(b) The solicitor should explain clearly to the client the time likely to be spent in dealing with a matter, if time spent is a factor in the calculation of the fees.

(c) Giving the best information possible includes:

- agreeing a fixed fee; or
- giving a realistic estimate; or
- giving a forecast within a possible range of costs; or explaining to the client the reasons why it is not possible to fix; or giving a realistic estimate or forecast of the overall

costs; and giving the best information possible about the cost of the next stage of the matter.

(d) The solicitor should, in an appropriate case, explain to a privately paying client that the client may set an upper limit on the firm's costs for which the client may be liable without further authority. Solicitors should not exceed an agreed limit without first obtaining the client's consent.

(e) The solicitor should make it clear at the outset if an estimate, quotation or other indication of cost is not intended to be fixed.

(f) The solicitor should also explain to the client how the firm's fees are calculated except where the overall costs are fixed or clear. If the basis of charging is an hourly charging rate, that must be made clear.

(g) The client should be told if charging rates may be increased.

(h) The solicitor should explain what reasonably foreseeable payments a client may have to make either to the solicitor or to a third party and when those payments are likely to be needed.

(i) The solicitor should explain to the client the arrangements for updating the costs information.

(j) The solicitor should discuss with the client how and when any costs are to be met, and consider:

- whether the client may be eligible and should apply for Legal Aid (including advice and assistance);
- whether the client's liability for his own costs may be covered by insurance;
- whether the client's liability for another party's costs may be covered by pre-purchased insurance and, if not, whether it would be advisable for the client's liability for another party's costs to be covered by after-the-event (ATE) insurance (including in every case where a conditional fee or contingency fee arrangement is proposed); and

- whether the client's liability for costs (including the costs of another party) may be paid by another person, for example, an employer or trade union.

(k) The solicitor should discuss with the client whether the likely outcome in a matter will justify the expense or risk involved including, if relevant, the risk of having to bear an opponent's costs.

Legally aided clients

(a) The solicitor should explain to a legally aided client the client's potential liability for the client's own costs and those of any other party, including:

 (i) the effect of the statutory charge and its likely amount;

 (ii) the client's obligation to pay any contribution assessed and the consequences of failing to do so;

 (iii) the fact that the client may still be ordered by the court to contribute to the opponent's costs if the case is lost even though the client's own costs are covered by Legal Aid; and

 (iv) the fact that even if the client wins, the opponent may not be ordered to pay or be capable of paying the full amount of the client's costs.

Privately paying clients in contentious matters (and potentially contentious matters)

The solicitor should explain to the client the client's potential liability for the client's own costs and for those of any other party, including:

(a) the fact that the client will be responsible for paying the firm's bill in full regardless of any order for costs made against an opponent;

(b) the probability that the client will have to pay the opponent's costs as well as the client's own costs if the case is lost;

(c) the fact that even if the client wins, the opponent may not be ordered to pay or be capable of paying the full amount of the client's costs; and

(d) the fact that if the opponent is legally aided the client may not recover costs, even if successful.

Liability for third party costs in non-contentious matters

The solicitor should explain to the client any liability the client may have for the payment of the costs of a third party. When appropriate, solicitors are advised to obtain a firm figure for or agree a cap to a third party's costs.

Updating costs information

The solicitor should keep the client properly informed about costs as a matter progresses. In particular, the solicitor should:

(a) tell the client, unless otherwise agreed, how much the costs are at regular intervals (at least every six months) and in appropriate cases deliver interim bills at agreed intervals;

(b) explain to the client (and confirm in writing) any changed circumstances which will or which are likely to affect the amount of costs, the degree of risk involved or the cost benefit to the client of continuing with the matter;

(c) inform the client in writing as soon as it appears that a costs estimate or agreed upper limit may or will be exceeded; and

(d) consider the client's eligibility for Legal Aid if a material change in the client's means comes to the solicitor's attention.

[source: *The Guide to the Professional Conduct of Solicitors*]

Alternative dispute resolution groups

Advertising Standards Authority
(Adverts – non-broadcast)
2 Torrington Place
London WC1E 7HW
Tel: 020 7580 5555
Fax: 020 7631 3051
Website: www.asa.org.uk

Covers print advertisements in newspapers or magazines, outdoor posters, direct mail leaflets and brochures, cinema advertisements, and advertisements on the Internet.

Air Transport Users Council
(Airlines – including lost luggage)
CAA House, 45-59 Kingsway
London WC2B 6TE
Tel: 020 7240 6061
Fax: 020 7240 7071
Website: www.caa.co.uk/auc

Covers airline passengers' disputes, including complaints about lost luggage.

Association of British Travel Agents
(Travel)
68-71 Newman Street
London W1T 3AH
Tel: 020 7637 2444
Fax: 020 7637 0713
Website: www.abta.com

Covers any dispute arising from any travel services provided by ABTA companies. This includes everything from the provision of information by travel agents to the quality of the holiday and accommodation provided by tour operators.

British Carpet Technical Centre
(Carpet cleaning)
BCTC-CAMRASO
Wira House, West Park Ring Road
Leeds LS16 6QL
Tel: 0113 259 1999

Covers carpet manufacturing defects.

Consumer Credit Trade Association
(Consumer credit)
Suite 8, The Wool Exchange
10 Hustlergate
Bradford BD1 1RE
Tel: 01274 390 380
Fax: 01274 729 002
Website: www.ccta.co.uk

Covers credit or hire agreements with individuals for other than business purposes within the financial limits of the Consumer Credit Act 1974, whether regulated by that Act or not.

Direct Selling Association
(Direct selling)
29 Floral Street
London WC2E 9DP
Tel: 020 7497 1234
Fax: 020 7497 3144
Website: www.dsa.org.uk

Covers the supply of consumer goods and services through independent direct sellers, primarily as a result of face-to-face contact with their customers away from business premises and usually in their homes.

Finance and Leasing Association
(Finance & leasing)
2nd Floor, Imperial House
15-19 Kingsway
London WC2B 6UN
Tel: 020 7836 6511
Fax: 020 7420 9600
Website: www.fla.org.uk

Applies to all credit or hire agreements made by customers with members of the FLA, whether they are regulated by the Consumer Credit Act 1974 or not.

Financial Ombudsman Service
(Banks & building societies, financial services, insurance & investment)
South Quay Plaza
183 Marsh Wall
London E14 9SR
Tel: 020 7964 1000
Consumer helpline: 0845 080 1800
Fax: 020 7964 1001
Website: www.financial-ombudsman.org.uk

Covers consumer complaints about financial firms that are regulated by the Financial Services Authority, and some unregulated firms after 1 December 2001. More specifically, personal financial matters: financial advice, banking services, insurance and investments.

Funeral Arbitration Scheme (National Association of Funeral Directors)
(Funerals)
618 Warwick Road
Solihull
West Midlands B91 1AA
Tel: 0845 230 1343

Fax: 0121 711 1351

Website: www.nafd.org.uk

Covers any aspect of the funeral service – provided by members.

Mail Order Traders' Association

(Mail order)
PO Box 1023
Liverpool L69 2WS
Tel: 0151 227 9456
Fax: 0151 227 9678

Covers firms that sell through catalogues. Members must follow their Code of Practice.

National Consumer Credit Federation

(Consumer credit)
98/100 Holme Lane
Sheffield S6 4JW
Tel: 0114 234 8101

Covers situations where customers' payments are collected from the home by a representative or agent.

Ombudsman for Estate Agents

(Estate agents)
Beckett House, 4 Bridge Street
Salisbury
Wiltshire SP1 2LX
Tel: 01722 333 306
Fax: 01722 332 296
Website: www.oea.co.uk

Covers estate agents where they have infringed someone's legal rights, treated someone unfairly, been inefficient or caused undue delay in a way that results in financial loss.

Pensions Ombudsman
(Pensions)
11 Belgrave Road
London SW1V 1RB
Tel: 020 7834 9144
Fax: 020 7821 0065
Website: www.pensions-ombudsman.org.uk

Covers injustice caused by maladministration of pension schemes.

Qualitas
(Furniture, floor coverings & allied trades)
Qualitas Conciliation Service
Qualitas Furnishing Standards
Maxwell Road
Stevenage SG1 2EW
Tel: 01438 777 777

Covers the purchase of furniture, floor coverings and allied trades.

Trading Standards Institute
(Faulty goods)
4/5 Hadleigh Business Centre
351 London Road
Hadleigh
Essex SS7 2BT
Tel: 0870 872 9000
Fax: 0870 872 9025
Website: www.tradingstandards.gov.uk

This site will put you in touch with your local authority Trading Standards Service. It also offer all sorts of useful information on a wide range of consumer issues. For example, there is advice on problems with buying goods, faulty goods, as well as difficulties with services (from dry-cleaning to going on holiday).

Contact details

Action for Victims of Medical Accidents
44 High Street
Croydon
Surrey CR0 1YB
Tel: 020 8686 8333
Fax: 020 8667 9065
Website: www.avma.org.uk

Association of Law Costs Draftsmen
Mrs S A Chapman
Church Cottage
Church Lane
Stuston, Diss
Norfolk IP21 4AG
Tel: 01379 741 404
Fax: 01379 742 702
Website: www.alcd.org.uk

Association of Personal Injury Lawyers
11 Castle Quay
Castle Boulevard
Nottingham NG7 1FW
Tel: 0115 958 0585
Fax: 0115 958 0885
Website: www.apil.com

Bar Council
3 Bedford Row
London WC1R 4DB
Tel: 020 7242 0082
Website: www.barcouncil.org.uk

British & Irish Ombudsman Association
24 Paget Gardens
Chislehurst
Kent BR7 5RX
Tel/Fax: 020 8467 7455
Website: www.bioa.org.uk

Chartered Institute of Arbitrators
International Arbitration Centre
12 Bloomsbury Square
London WC1A 2LP
Tel: 020 7421 7444
Fax: 020 7404 4023
Website: www.arbitrators.org

Compensation Fund
Victoria Court
8 Dormer Place
Leamington Spa
Warwickshire CV32 5AE
Tel: 01926 820 082
Fax: 01926 431 435

Complaints Commissioner
General Council of the Bar
Northumberland House
305-306 High Holborn
London WC1V 7JZ
Tel: 020 7440 4000
Fax: 020 7440 4001
Website: www.barcouncil.org.uk

Consumers' Association
2 Marylebone Road
London NW1 4DF
Tel: 020 7486 5544
Website: www.which.net

Council for Licensed Conveyancers
16 Glebe Road
Chelmsford
Essex CM1 1QG
Tel: 01245 349 599
Fax: 01245 341 300
Website: www.conveyancer.org.uk

Department for Constitutional Affairs
(formerly known as the Lord Chancellor's Department)
Selborne House, 54-60 Victoria Street
London SW1E 6QW
Tel: 020 7210 8500
Website: www.lcd.gov.uk

Employment Lawyers Association
PO Box 353
Uxbridge UB10 0UN
Tel/Fax: 01895 256 972
Website: www.elaweb.org.uk

Free Representation Unit
4th Floor, Peer House
8-14 Verulam Street
London WC1X 8LZ
Tel: 020 7831 0692
Website: www.fru.org.uk

Immigration Law Practitioners' Association

Lindsey House, 40-42 Charterhouse Street
London EC1M 6JN
Tel: 020 7251 8383
Fax: 020 7251 8384
Website: www.ilpa.org.uk

Insolvency Service

21 Bloomsbury Street
London WC1B 3QW
Tel: 020 7291 6895
Website: www.insolvency.gov.uk

Institute of Legal Executives

Kempston Manor
Kempston
Bedfordshire MK42 7AB
Tel: 01234 841 000
Fax: 01234 840 373
Website: www.ilex.org.uk

Law Centres Federation

Duchess House, 18-19 Warren Street
London W1T 5LR
Tel: 020 7387 8570
Fax: 020 7387 8368
Website: www.lawcentres.org.uk

Law Society of England & Wales

113 Chancery Lane
London WC2A 1PL
Tel: 020 7242 1222
Website: www.lawsociety.org.uk

Legal Services Commission
85 Gray's Inn Road
London WC1X 8TX
Tel: 020 7759 0000
Website: www.legalservices.gov.uk

Legal Services Ombudsman
3rd Floor, Sunlight House
Quay Street
Manchester M3 3JZ
Tel: 0161 839 7262
Fax: 0161 832 5446
Website: www.olso.org

Liberty
21 Tabard Street
London SE1 4LA
Tel: 020 7403 3888
Fax: 020 7407 5354
Website: www.liberty-human-rights.org.uk

Mediation UK
Alexander House, Telephone Avenue
Bristol BS1 4BS
Tel: 0117 904 6661
Fax: 0117 904 3331
Website: www.mediationuk.org.uk

Motor Accident Solicitors Society
54 Baldwin Street
Bristol BS1 1QW
Tel: 0117 929 2560
Fax: 0117 904 7220
Website: www.mass.org.uk

National Association of Citizens Advice Bureaux
Myddleton House, 115-123 Pentonville Road
London N1 9LZ
Tel: 020 7833 2181
Website: www.nacab.org.uk
Website: www.adviceguide.org.uk

Office for the Supervision of Solicitors
Victoria Court, 8 Dormer Place
Leamington Spa
Warwickshire CV32 5AE
Tel: 01926 820 082
Helpline: 0845 608 6565
Fax: 01926 431 435
Website: www.oss.lawsociety.org.uk

Registry Trust Limited
173-175 Cleveland Street
London WIP 5PE
Tel: 020 7380 0133
Website: www.registry-trust.org.uk

Shelter
88 Old Street
London EC1V 9HU
Helpline: 0808 800 4444
Tel: 020 7505 4699
Fax: 020 7505 2030
Website: www.shelter.org.uk

Solicitors Disciplinary Tribunal
3rd Floor, Gate House
1 Farringdon Street
London EC4M 7NS

Tel: 020 7329 4808
Fax: 020 7329 4833
Website: www.solicitorstribunal.org.uk

Solicitors Family Law Association

PO Box 302
Orpington
Kent BR6 8QX
Tel: 01689 850 227
Fax: 01689 855 833
Website: www.sfla.org.uk

Solicitors Pro Bono Group

1 Pudding Lane
London EC3R 8AB
Tel: 0870 777 5601
Website: www.probonogroup.org.uk

Glossary

This is a jargon-buster explaining legal terms that commonly arise in connection with lawyers, the courts and legal costs.

after-the-event (ATE) insurance – a form of legal expenses insurance that, as the name suggests, covers a policyholder for an event that has already happened. It works with a conditional fee agreement (CFA). Under a CFA, generally if you are successful your opponent pays the legal costs. If you are not, you will not have to pay your solicitor's costs but you will be exposed to the other side's costs. Many policies will cover this cost plus a range of other expenses including, for example, medical costs, court fees or barristers' charges. As an alternative to conditional fee insurance, your solicitor may work for you on a normal basis where you will have to pay him whether you win or lose. To protect you from costs, however, he may offer you both sides costs (BSC) insurance covering both your own and your opponent's solicitor's fees and other costs whether you win or lose.

alternative dispute resolution (ADR) – a term that covers the various methods that can be used to settle a dispute without going to trial, such as arbitration and mediation.

arbitration – an informal means of arriving at a decision on a dispute that is binding on both parties. Many trade bodies have arbitration schemes operated by independent bodies, such as the Chartered Institute for Arbitrators. (Actions before the Small Claims Court are also called arbitration, which reflects a more relaxed consumer-friendly version of the courts).

barrister – a lawyer who appears in the higher courts to plead or argue a case. He is advised by his instructing solicitor.

before-the-event (BTE) insurance – a form of legal expenses insurance that protects you against the costs of bringing or defending a legal action. It can be purchased as a standalone policy but is more commonly sold (or given away) alongside motor policies and home policies.

civil law – part of the law relating to people's rights and agreements between individuals (as opposed to criminal law). Generally, it involves the dispute over property, commercial transactions or family matters such as divorce and adoption. The main areas of civil law are tort (which includes negligence and nuisance) and contract.

claimant – a person (or business) who brings a legal action (previously known as a 'plaintiff').

conditional fee agreement (CFA) – a funding arrangement that is more commonly called 'no win, no fee' (NWNF). Under a CFA, a solicitor is allowed to charge you a sum (known as the 'success fee') to reward his risk of not being paid should he lose. ATE insurance is available to protect you from the other side's costs if you lose. If you win, the cost of the success fee and insurance policy can be recovered from the losing party. Although such arrangements are known as NWNF, you can strike a no win, low fee arrangement where, for example, your solicitor charges half the hourly rate if unsuccessful.

contentious – covers legal action that goes through the courts. Work becomes contentious when court proceedings have actually begun. By contrast, examples of non-contentious work include conveyancing, drafting Wills, as well as negotiating contracts.

contingency fees – another form of NWNF, *see* conditional fee agreements. However, they are far more straightforward as the solicitor takes his fees as a straight percentage of the award. They are generally limited to non-contentious actions.

contract – a legal agreement between two or more parties. A contract does not have to be in writing, and words do not even have to be exchanged.

conveyancing – law and procedure relating to the purchase and sale of a property.

County court – one of the types of courts in England and Wales that hears local civil cases. County courts deal with a wide range of different types of cases, but the most common ones are landlord and tenant disputes, consumer disputes, personal injury claims, undefended divorce cases, some domestic violence cases (can also be heard in the magistrates' court), employment and race and sex discrimination cases.

Court of Appeal – deals with civil and criminal appeals in England and Wales. Civil appeals from the High Court and the County court are dealt with, as well as from the Employment Appeal Tribunal and the Lands Tribunal. Criminal appeals include appeals against convictions in the Crown Court, as well as appeals on particular points of law.

criminal law – part of the law concerned with illegal acts committed against individuals or society as a whole (as opposed to civil law). Criminal law uses the power of the courts to seek punishment for these offences and is primarily concerned with punishment, deterrence and rehabilitation.

Crown Court – more senior in the criminal justice system than the magistrates' court. It deals with more serious criminal cases heard by judge and jury, appeals from the magistrates' court, and convictions that are referred to the Crown Court for sentencing.

damages – money claimed by a claimant from a defendant as compensation for harm done, as well as money awarded by the court as compensation to a claimant.

defendant – a person (or business) who has legal proceedings brought against them.

disbursements – expenses that have to be paid in connection with a case. For example, court fees or fees paid to the Land Registry.

the European Court of Human Rights – sits in Strasbourg and deals with cases in which a person thinks their human rights have been contravened and for which there is no legal remedy within the national legal system.

the European Court of Justice – sits in Luxembourg and advises on the interpretation of European Community law and takes action against infringements. There are 15 judges, one from each member state.

expert witness – a person with special skills, technical knowledge or professional qualifications, who is generally independent of the parties.

High Court – the main civil court that sits at the Royal Courts of Justice in London and other centres throughout England and Wales. It is divided into three divisions covering different areas of law: Queen's Bench (general civil claims for tort and contract); Chancery (Wills, inheritance, tax, companies, liquidation, bankruptcy, etc); and Family (family matters).

House of Lords – the highest court that deals mainly with appeals from the Court of Appeal, or direct from the High Court, where the case involves a point of law of general public importance. Appeals are mostly civil cases, although the five Law Lords do deal with some criminal appeals.

judgment – the formal decision of the court.

judicial review – a legal procedure for applying to the court to deal with the abuse of power by public bodies.

legal executive – a qualified lawyer specialising in a particular area of law. He will have passed the Institute of Legal Executives' professional qualification in that particular area.

legal expenses insurance – a term that covers both ATE insurance and BTE insurance.

licensed conveyancer – a specialist property lawyer who advises the public on conveyancing and is a member of the Council for Licensed Conveyancers.

litigant-in-person – a person who represents himself before the courts.

litigation – the act of taking legal action against someone or something. The person who begins this legal action is called the litigant.

magistrates' courts – the lowest courts in the criminal justice system that deal with criminal and some civil cases. Cases are dealt with either by Justices of the Peace, who are not legally qualified but have a qualified clerk to advise them on the law, or by District Judges, who are qualified lawyers. They deal with criminal offences where the defendant is not entitled to trial by jury or decides against it. Magistrates also deal with civil cases, such as debts, the granting of licences for pubs and clubs, some family matters (such as maintenance and removing a spouse from the matrimonial home) and the welfare of children.

mediation – a process outside a court of law that resolves a dispute between two or more parties. Using legal referees, called mediators, the parties involved agree to come to some kind of solution without embarking on the costly process of going to court.

negligence – the breach of a legal duty to take reasonable care, resulting in damage to the claimant.

no win, no fee (NWNF) – this covers those kinds of funding arrangements with lawyers where, as the name implies, they are not paid if they are unsuccessful. It is an umbrella term that covers CFAs and contingency fees.

nuisance – the unlawful interference with someone else's enjoyment of his property.

ombudsman – an official appointed to investigate complaints by the public against government departments or professional organisations. He provides an independent and impartial means of resolving certain disputes outside the courts.

paralegal – undertakes legal work without any formal qualification, usually under the supervision of a qualified lawyer.

rights of audience – the entitlement to appear before a court as a lawyer and conduct proceedings on behalf of a party. Until recently, barristers had a monopoly on the right to represent clients in the higher courts. However, since 1994, solicitors are entitled to the same rights of audience after training.

Small Claims Court – a civil process that resolves legal disputes in which the claimant claims a small sum of money (up to £5,000 generally, and up to £1,000 in personal injury cases). It takes place in the County court and the usual court formalities are dispensed with.

solicitor – a lawyer who is a member of the Law Society. He will have passed his exams, should be in receipt of a valid practising certificate (without which he cannot practice) and provide advice to members of the public and represent them.

solicitor-advocate – a solicitor who is experienced and qualified to represent individuals before the higher courts.

tort – a civil wrong committed against a person for which compensation may be sought through a civil court, for example, personal injury, negligent driving or libel.

tribunal – an informal court, usually with a lawyer as a chairman plus two lay members.

Index